3D
Fashion
Design

3D

Fashion Design

Technique, design and visualization

Thomas Makryniotis

BATSFORD

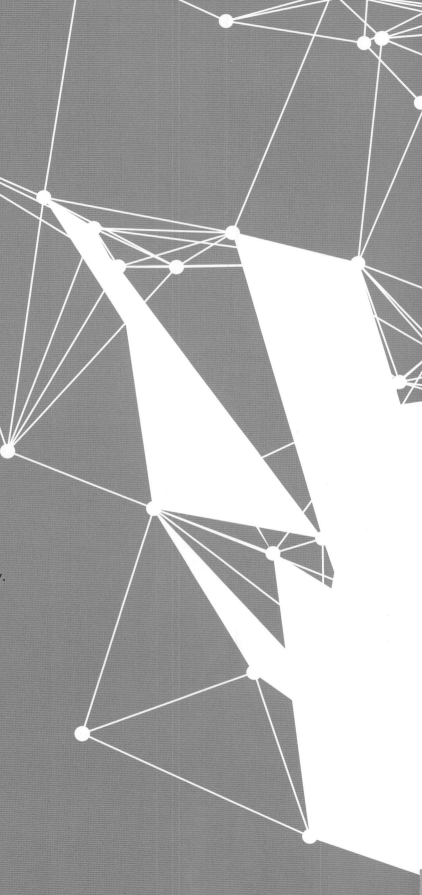

First published in the United Kingdom in 2015
by Batsford
1 Gower Street, London WC1E 6HD

An imprint of Pavilion Books Company Ltd

ISBN 9781849942935

A CIP catalogue record for this book is available from the British Library.

10 9 8 7 6 5 4 3 2 1

Reproduction by Rival colour UK
Printed and bound by 1010 Printing International Ltd, China

This book can be ordered direct from
the publisher at www.pavilionbooks.com.

I would like to thank Gabrielle Miller, Zowie Broach, Anne Valerie Hash,
Raphaëlle Mura, Henri Mura, and Philip Delamore for their valuable
contribution to this book.

Contents

Introduction

Fashion is a late adopter of technology. Although it relies on innovation, due to the size of the industry and for socio-economic reasons, new technologies have taken time to spread and to establish themselves as industry standards or common practices. Gradually, however, 3D graphics, virtual reality, and other relevant digital technologies have begun to migrate from electronic entertainment and visual effects to several different aspects of fashion. They are being used in fashion design in the form of Computer-aided Design (CAD) and product development and visualization. They are also being used in promotion – see, for example, Prada's clothes based on *Final Fantasy* characters for the *Arena Homme+* magazine, as well as Prada's *Trembled Blossoms* film short.

They have been used in navigable 3D spaces for e-tail (American Apparel in *Second Life*, the H&M expansion for *The Sims* 2, the Diesel store in PlayStation®Home, the Stylemee shop city prototype) and for curation (Valentino Garavani Museum).

In all of these applications, with the advancement of technology, we move increasingly from abstract representation to realistic depiction, towards photorealistic and physically accurate bodies and clothes.

This book is the first of its kind, describing some of the techniques and workflow used in the fashion industry for 3D product prototyping, development and visualization. It is structured as a set of tutorials, describing some of the basic processes used in 3D visualization for fashion, progressing from beginner to intermediate level. Some of the most advanced elements of the processes have been deliberately omitted, so that they do not pose a disproportionate challenge to the reader. The tutorials are laid out as sets of screenshots depicting the processes together with accompanying text describing each step in detail.

The digital revolution and its impact on the fashion industry

Digital technologies are now used in many aspects of the fashion industry. One of the main areas is the delivery of products, user interaction with these products, and their fitting on avatars.

Anthropometrics is a research field based on collecting real-world data for the purpose of creating 3D body models on computers. It is useful for the modelling of bodies through the use of global body data surveys and the listing of parameters (parametric avatars), as well as for for the creation of 3D models from 3D body scans. Once the 3D bodies have been recreated, they can be animated with motion capture data, where recorded performances of actors are applied to the skeletons of the digital bodies.

The modelling and digitizing of fabric materials is another area of interest. Fabrics can be recreated on the computer through the use of algorithms, or, as is most often the case, they can be photographed, retouched, and repeated over the surface of a 3D garment. The development and use of Shaders (sets of commands that change the appearance of a 3D surface) is a long-standing principle of 3D digital design, and it is crucial for the purposes of fashion, where the realistic representation of fabrics is important.

Then of course there is the construction of the garments themselves through CAD. Digital fashion design software, such as CLO3D, Optitex PDS, and Browzwear V-Stitcher, are used extensively today for product development. Cloth simulation is usually applied within the fashion CAD software, although there are also external cloth physics engines, such as Maya's nCloth, Numerion's Carbon and FXGear's Qualoth. These engines can often accept real-world data from Cloth Mechanical Properties Measurement Systems such as Kawabata and FAST, which makes the replication of existing materials possible.

The 3D content produced within fashion CAD can then be used in several different applications, pre-rendered (film and stills) or real-time, such as e-commerce web interfaces, navigable 3D stores and exhibitions, interactive apps and augmented reality. The film and video games industries are also increasingly using fashion CAD to create and simulate the clothing of characters, and to include it in 3D scenes or mix it with live video footage. On the other hand, 3D content such as jewellery and accessories, developed with product prototyping software such as Rhino3D, may be 3D printed for product testing and proof-of-concept purposes.

There are undoubtedly many benefits that come with 3D technologies: ease of collaboration between team members as well as between professional and client, efficiency of product development, customer engagement through the interaction with products, and the easy customization of products, are just few of these benefits. Sustainability is also improved through the reduction of physical prototyping and production samples, and through the consumption of virtual products. Furthermore, the same 3D content can be used for visualization, e-tailing and marketing purposes, further reducing costs.

Perhaps important from a philosophical perspective is that through fashion, the digital body now exists for the first time. We have moved from the modelling of permanent clothes on a character's 3D surface (texturing on a single polygon shell), to physically accurate garment draping and fitting on a pre-existing body. This entails the expression of identities in a virtual society through virtual products. But this is not a philosophy book ...

Fashion-specific 3D software

The traditional kind of software for the fashion industry has been pattern-cutting Software. Gerber has become synonymous with fashion CAD, and there are other companies that provide excellent solutions, such as Assyst, Optitex and Lectra. This is the software that deals with the development of 2D patterns for the construction of garments, physical or digital. Patterns are either constructed with analogue methods and digitized, or made exclusively with digital methods, usually based on the alteration of standard pattern blocks.

The 2D patterns are then input in 3D fashion software, such as CLO3D, Optitex PDS, and Browzwear V-Stitcher, where the 2D patterns are placed on a 3D mannequin, sewn and fitted on the body. The garments are draped around the body by use of cloth simulation based on cloth mechanical properties measurement systems such as Kawabata and FAST.

Generic 3D software that can be used for fashion

Apart from fashion-specific software, the fashion industry is also starting to make use of generic 3D modelling and animation software, which was originally developed for other industry sectors, such as product design, architecture, and visual effects. First up, there are the general 3D packages such as Autodesk Maya, Autodesk 3ds Max, The Foundry's MODO, and McNeel's Rhino3D. Then there are character animation packages like Autodesk's Motionbuilder and online services such as Ikinema Webanimate and Mixamo. Rendering software such as Octane, V-Ray, Maxwell, Arnold, Mental Ray and Iray is used to reproduce renders of 3D scenes based on photorealistic lighting, and it is increasingly used for fashion purposes. Finally, there are external cloth physics engines by companies such as Numerion, FXGear, and Vidya. Most generic 3D packages also feature their own cloth simulation features, as part of their wider physics engines. Maya nCloth, for example, is part of Maya's nucleus physics system, which also includes water, smoke, hair, and fur.

Workflow

The 3D fashion visualization pipeline can be summarized in the following stages: avatar creation; avatar animation; 2D pattern creation; creation of materials and textures; garment construction and draping; scene composition (including avatar, garments, hair simulation, lights, cameras, and application of materials); and rendering and compositing.

Here is what a typical 3D fashion visualization pipeline looks like:

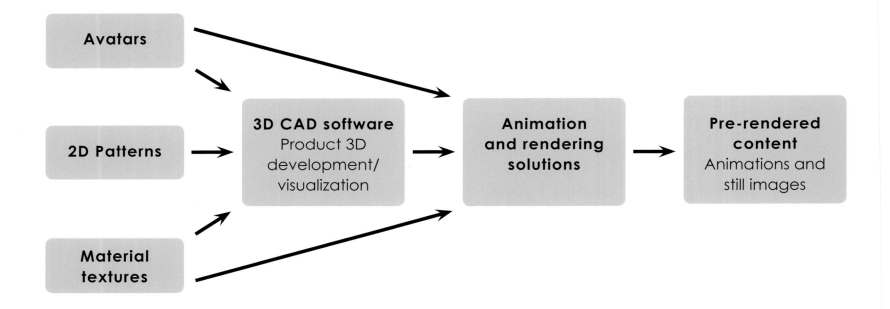

The principles of 3D

All 3D work takes place in 3D Space, which is based on an XYZ coordinate system. There are three axes: the X axis for width, the Y axis for height and the Z axis for depth. Time could be regarded as a fourth dimension, as animation takes place over several frames, where specific attributes, such as position and rotation are 'keyframed'. Character rigs (skeletons) are also controlled in this way. Apart from X, Y and Z, there are also the local U and V dimensions of a surface, which are used for the placement of bitmap textures on surfaces, in order to add colour, bump, displacement, and transparency.

There is usually a perspective view, which allows you to visualize 3D space from a freely moveable camera, based on the camera's position and the viewing angle. Orthographic views, on the other hand, work on only two axes at a time, for accuracy. Both kinds of view are important in 3D work. The shading of the viewpoints usually varies from wireframe (just lines) to fully rendered (IPR hardware rendering).

In 3D space, one may manipulate whole objects or their components. These may be connected in a hierarchical parent-child relationship, and there usually is a graph window (Maya has the Outliner) where these relationships are listed. There are tools, called 'manipulators', that facilitate the movement, scaling, and rotation of objects and components, based on colour-coded handles for the three different axes.

There are several types of 3D geometry, but polygons are the most common. This is what we will use in this book as it is the most appropriate for the kind of work that we will be carrying out. Polygons consist of vertices (points in 3D space), edges (lines between pairs of vertices), faces (made up of three or more edges) and UVs (2D coordinates for the display of texture bitmaps on a mesh). Common polygon operations include extruding faces, splitting polygons, and joining objects with Boolean commands.

The Shading of a model (in our case polygon meshes) defines how its geometry reacts to light. Material qualities are described in material nodes, and they are used to apply specific materials to parts of models. The Diffuse and Specular attributes are most common, controlling the colour and shine of a surface. Others control details such as Bumps, Displacement and Transparency. Shading largely depends on the lighting setup of a scene. There are several kinds of lights depending on the software, which may include spot lights, directional lights, point lights, area lights, volume lights, and HDRI (high dynamic range image based lighting). As most renderers today use ray-tracing or path-tracing techniques, shadows are automatically calculated. During rendering, a 2D bitmap is produced based on the current scene's components, i.e. the geometry, lights and materials from a specific camera's point of view.

Creating the mannequin

Creating the mannequin with Daz Studio

The first project is to build a fashion model to wear our designs. We will use a programme called Daz Studio, a programme for human modelling and animation; it is free to download and runs on both PCs and Macs. The interface is laid out in a way that allows the easy application of poses, movements, props, clothing, hair, materials, and other content to the human model. The standard installation includes many options, but you can also download content from the Daz store (www.daz3D.com). There are also many different presets for the interface layout, but here I will be using the default preset. In this tutorial we will create, adjust, pose and export a fashion model from Daz Studio for use in other 3D programmes, such as Marvelous Designer and Maya.

Interface + plugins

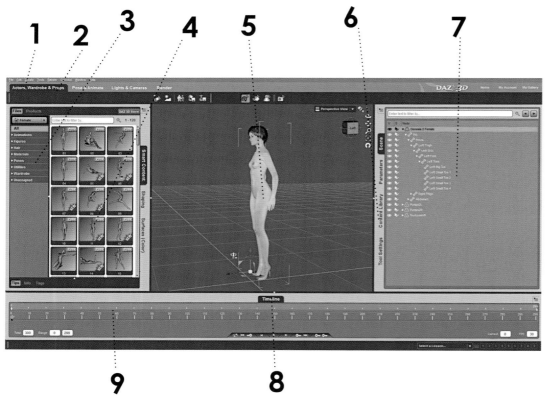

1 The main menu - This is where all of the commands can be found, separated into categories.

2 Activity bar - This allows you to switch between interface elements.

3 Content categories – These are categories for finding content such as mannequins and props.

4 Content icons – These display a preview of the content.

5 3D viewport – This is where the 3D content is placed and manipulated.

6 Scene, parameters, content, and tool tabs – These are tabs that contain options for various elements of a scene.

7 Scene hierarchy - All of the scene elements and their relationships are listed here and can also be selected.

8 Timeline and Animate tabs.

9 Timeline and AniMate panels – These allow you to switch between Timeline and AniMate.

10 Actor's parameters panel – This includes sliders that affect the shape of the mannequin.

11 Pose controls panel – This includes sliders that affect the pose of the mannequin.

12 Content library – This includes the available content for use in a scene.

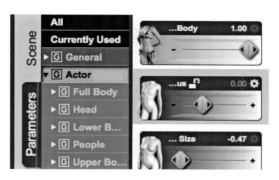

1 Expand the right palette and click on the Content Library tab. Chose a model to load onto the scene – I chose Victoria 6 (DAZ Studio Formats > My DAZ 3D Library > People > Genesis 2 Female > Characters). Other models may be installed at other locations, and their makers normally include instructions for installation and use.

2 Daz includes detailed controls for the shaping of the model's body in the Parameters tab of the right panel, in the Actor section. Feel free to experiment by dragging the sliders that correspond to the several body sections. You can expand the Actor hierarchy to find specific body parts and edit them, such as Upper Body > Chest.

3 Now, we need to put a pair of shoes on our model. Although we can locate shoes in the panels on both sides of the interface, it is sometimes easier to browse through content in the left panel. Under the Smart Content tab, and in the Wardrobe > Footwear section, you will find the installed footwear. In this example, I double-click on Pumps 2 for Victoria 6 to put them on the model.

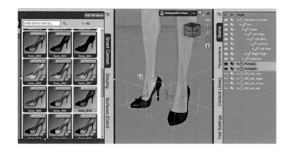

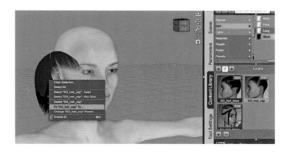

4 Select both shoes in the Scene tab of the right panel. Most content developers include several material options for their props. In the Materials section of the Smart Content tab, I browsed through the different material options for the Pumps 2 shoes, and double-clicked the green and black option to apply it.

5 In some cases, the shoes do not conform to the model's feet correctly, and some developers include utilities to help with this. In the Content Library, under DAZ Studio Formats > My DAZ 3D Library > People > Genesis 2 Female > Clothing > dx30 > Pumps2 > Poses, I have a FootSet icon, which sets the feet at the right angle for the particular shoes. Select the Victoria model and double-click on the icon.

6 In Categories > Default > Hair, click on a hairstyle – I am using Stalker Girl, which comes in four parts (cap, base, fringe, and tail). As Stalker Girl is made for older Genesis figures, Daz offers an Auto-Fit dialogue. I chose Genesis as its original destination, and Long Hair as its type, then I selected Fit "SG_hair_cap" To: Genesis 2 Female. The rest of the hair parts will automatically conform to the cap.

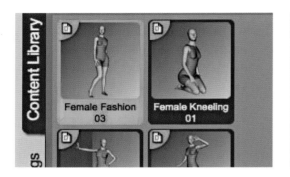

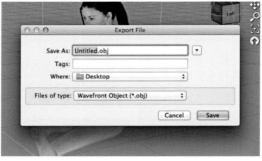

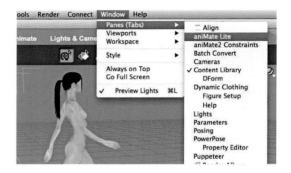

7 Next we will pose the model using pre-made poses in the Content Library. All Daz poses, pre-installed and purchased third-party ones, should work with Victoria 6. Explore different poses and pose the model for our initial export, which will be a static model for draping for a still render. I found my pose under DAZ Studio Formats > My DAZ 3D Library > People > Genesis 2 Female > Poses. Poses can also be tweaked or created from scratch using the posing sliders in the Parameters tab, under Pose Controls.

8 Let us now save our scene by going to File > Save As > Scene. Let us also go to File > Export. In the Export File dialogue, select Wavefront Object (.obj) for type, name the file, and hit Save. This format is an exchange standard that includes geometry and materials, but no animation.

9 To export an animated figure, we must first animate our model. For this, we will use the panel that we hid before, the Timeline, along with another panel called aniMate Lite. To turn on the latter, go to the Window menu and select Panes(Tabs) > aniMate Lite. aniMate is a panel that allows you to drag into it blocks of premade animations to create longer sequences.

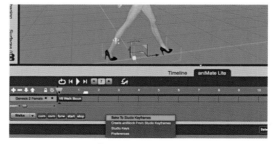

10 There are some blocks included with Daz, but in this example I am using a fashion walk by Skamotion (the place to find aniMate blocks is DAZ Studio Formats > My DAZ 3D Library > aniBlocks). Simply double-clicking on the block icon will add it to the aniMate panel. Blocks can be lined up and repeated, and they can also be rearranged just by clicking and dragging them in the aniMate timeline. Play around with the blocks until you have an animation sequence you are happy with.

11 Before we can export our animation for use in a draping program like Marvelous Designer, we must convert the aniMate blocks to keyframes in our timeline. To do this, right-click near the bottom of the aniMate panel, and from the pop-up window select 'Bake To Studio Keyframes'. Say yes to the dialogue to confirm the transfer of the blocks to keyframes. Click on the Timeline tab to see the transferred keyframes on it – represented as small black triangles.

12 We are now ready to save the walk animation by going to File > Export and selecting the Autodesk FBX format in Files of Type, which is used to store geometry, materials, and skeletal animation.

Creating garments

Creating a Raphaëlle Mura outfit

In the second project, we will replicate an existing garment in 3D using a program called Marvelous Designer, a cut-down version of CLO3D, an industrial piece of software for garment design and cloth simulation. Marvelous Designer is increasingly used in many industries, including visual effects, film, video games, and fashion. It allows for on-the-fly manipulation of 2D patterns on a 3D mannequin, and therefore for very fast product prototyping and development. In the following tutorial, we will go over basic techniques for creating fashion designs and draping them around a mannequin with full cloth simulation. The tutorials can be downloaded from the website listed in Resources (page 173).

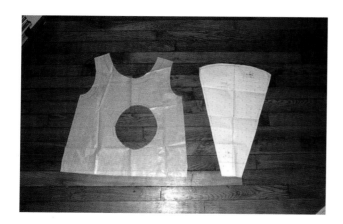

Preparation of photographs and patterns

In this tutorial, we will attempt to digitally reconstruct a design by Raphaëlle Mura, whose photographs will act as references for our digital patterns. Photographic reference of garments and fashion patterns usually has inherent problems, such as perspective distortion due to the position of the camera during photographing, and brightness and contrast issues due to the lighting conditions. We will therefore use Photoshop, the most established image manipulation software, to edit the available reference photos. We will then use Illustrator, the most prominent vector graphics software, to trace the photographed patterns, so that we can then convert them to a format that Marvelous Designer can understand.

Photoshop interface

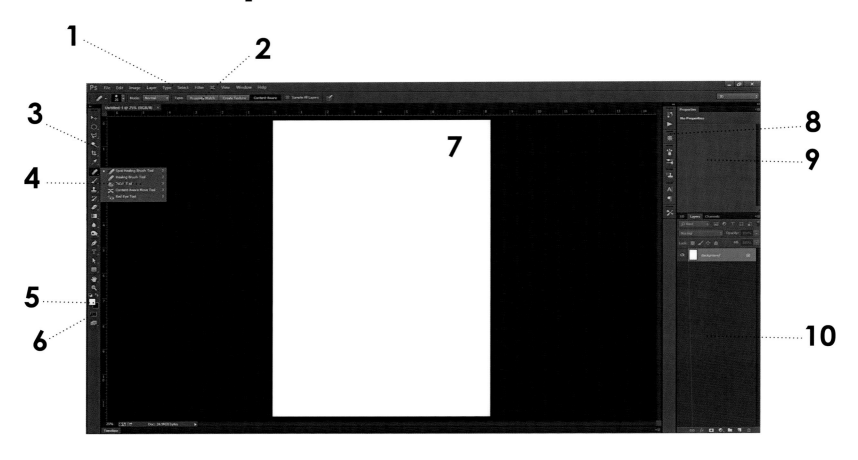

1 The main menu – This is where all of the commands can be found, separated into categories.

2 Tool options bar – This options bar offers various options for each tool.

3 Main toolbar – This is where all of Photoshop's tools are kept.

4 Tool category pop-up menu – Clicking and holding on a tool icon with a triangle in its corner will bring up a menu with more similar tools.

5 Foreground and background colours – These are the colours of choice for painting and erasing.

6 Quick mask mode switch – This switches between normal and quick mask modes.

7 Canvas – The canvas is the extents of the document.

8 Docked palettes – These are collapsible palettes that deal with various processes.

9 Properties palette – Displays information on selected tools and objects.

10 Layers palette – Displays and allows the manipulation of document layers.

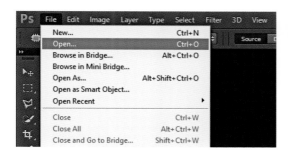

1 In Photoshop, go to File > Open. Locate and open the first photograph.

2 Go to Layer > New > Layer. In the New Layer dialogue, just hit OK. This will create a new blank layer on top of the existing layer containing the photograph.

3 Now double-click on the photograph layer (background layer) in the Layers palette to unlock it. We must do this in order to be able to manipulate the photograph as a separate layer. Click and drag the photograph layer over the empty layer in the Layers palette.

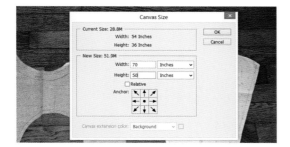

4 Under the Image menu, select Canvas Size. The current canvas size is 54x36 inches. Change it to 70x50 inches. There is now enough extra space to allow us to manipulate the photograph.

5 Click inside the rulers and drag towards the document to create horizontal and vertical guides to help you with aligning the photograph. If the rulers are off, you can turn them on by going to View > Rulers.

6 Go to Edit > Transform > Perspective and use the Perspective tool on the edges of the image to skew it.

7 Go to Edit > Transform > Distort and drag the corner handles of the image so its contents become as flat as possible.

8 Select the Crop tool and drag the document bounds inwards to trim the image.

9 File > Save As to save the image in Photoshop or as JPEG format to use in Illustrator (select the highest JPEG quality).

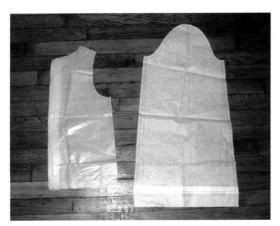

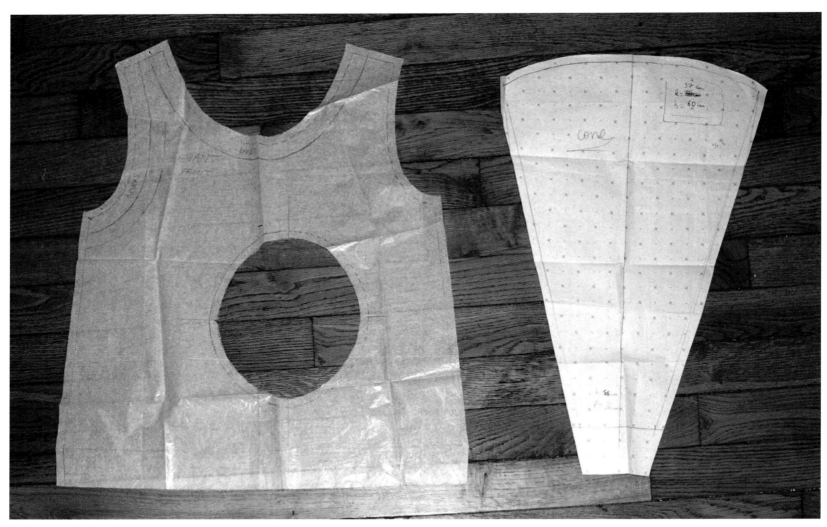

10 Final patterns: this is what the edited photographs should look like.

Illustrator interface

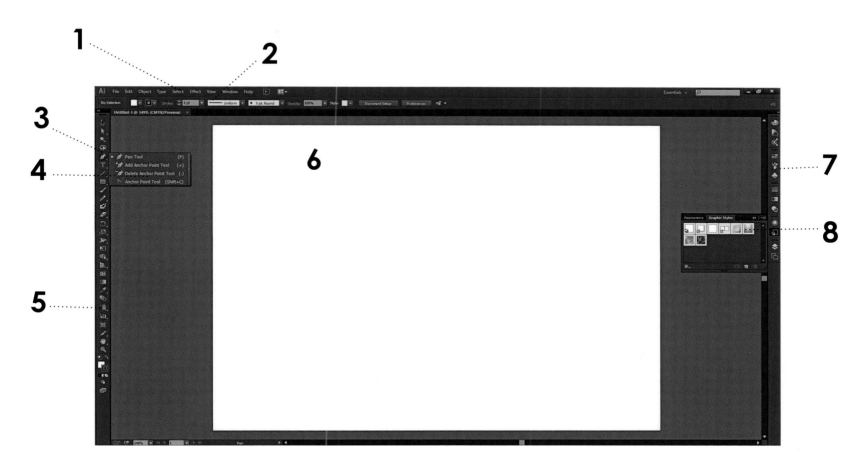

1 Main menu – This is where all of the commands can be found, separated into categories.

2 Tool options bar – This options bar offers various options for each tool.

3 Main toolbar – This is where all of Illustrator's tools are kept.

4 Tool category pop-up menu – Clicking and holding on a tool icon with a triangle in its corner will bring up a menu with more similar tools.

5 Outline and fill colours – These are the colours of choice for outlines and fills.

6 Artboard – The artboard is the extents of the document. Multiple artboards can be used at the same time.

7 Docked palettes – These are collapsible palettes that deal with various processes.

8 Expanded styles palette – Expanded palettes contain various options and functions. In this case, object styles.

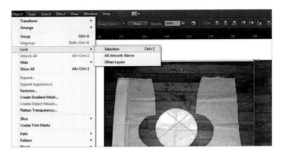

1 Next, we need to trace the photographs in Illustrator to create the DXF patterns that can be imported into CLO3D. Go to File > New and create a landscape A4 document, although the exact size does not matter much here, as the exported DXF patterns will be resized in CLO3D.

2 Now go to File > Place. Locate and open the edited photographs. Lay them out on the document approximately at the same size – drag the corner handles of the bounding boxes of the photos while holding SHIFT to change their size.

3 Shift-click on all three photos to select them all and go to Object > Lock > Selection to lock them in place so that they cannot be accidentally moved.

4 Click on the Stroke icon and select black from the colour picker. Click on the Fill icon and make sure it is transparent by clicking on the small white rectangle with the diagonal red line, which is located right below the Stroke icon.

5 Pick the Pen tool and start tracing the first pattern, making sure to leave a 1cm distance from the edge – the patterns include seam allowance but it is not needed for the patterns to be used in CLO3D. Click and release once to place the first point, then click and release again for the next point to create a line; or click, drag and release to create a curve. This tool is one of the best Illustrator tools, but it takes a while to get to grips with. Continue tracing around the pattern and finally close the shape by clicking on the first point.

6 Now pick the Direct Selection (white arrow) tool that is used for selecting and moving components, and refine the shape by repositioning some of the points and the tangency handles on curves (handles that control the shape of the curve, which appear upon clicking on a curve point) to make the shape smoother.

 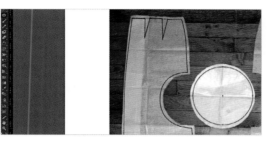 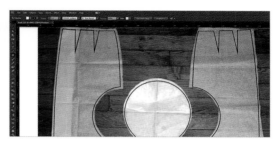

7 Pick the Convert Anchor Point tool, which can be found in the Pen tool submenu (click and hold on the Pen to open the submenu). This can be used to further refine curves by dragging the tangency handles independently rather than in pairs. It also converts corners to curves, by clicking on a corner point and dragging, and curves to corners by just clicking on a curve point.

8 Pick up the Ellipse tool, click at the centre of the circular pattern and drag while pressing SHIFT and ALT on the keyboard to create a perfect circle with its centre at the centre of the pattern. SHIFT makes the ellipse a circle, and ALT starts the drawing of the circle from its centre rather than from its side. You can drag guides from the rulers and position them on the document to help you with the alignment of lines, although they are not necessary.

9 We will now duplicate and mirror the first shape. Select the shape and go to Edit > Copy and then Edit > Paste in Front. With the copy selected, pick up the Reflect tool from the Rotate tool menu (click and hold), click once to position the anchor point (mirror plane) for the reflection, and then click anywhere and drag clockwise to rotate the shape so that it is positioned opposite the original. Holding SHIFT will constrain the rotation to every 45 degrees, making it easier to make the reflected piece at 180 degrees from the original.

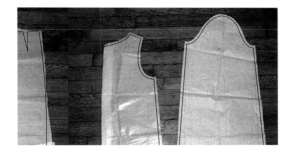 

10 Continue to trace the back of the top and the sleeve, as well as the front of the top and its decoration.

11 With all of the patterns traced, all that remains is to export the patterns in DXF format for use in CLO3D. Go to File > Export and select AutoCAD Interchange File (*.DXF) under Save As Type, then name and save your DXF. You may also want to File > Save As to also save the file in Illustrator format for further editing later.

Format conversion

Although the patterns are now traced and exported from Illustrator as DXF files, fashion-specific software such as Marvelous Designer can only read a special kind of DXF, which is called DXF-AAMA. We will therefore need to convert the DXFs to DXF-AAMAs. There are a few ways of doing this but we will use the Optitex PDS software in this example. In the following tutorial, we will import our DXF patterns into PDS and export them as DXF-AAMAs by using the built-in format conversion utility. We will then use CLO3D to covert the DXF-AAMAs to Marvelous Designer projects. CLO3D is very simillar to Marvelous, with some additional advanced functionality such as pattern import. This is why we are using CLO3D to import our patterns. CLO3D is an industrial, and therefore expensive solution, but an easy alternative to importing patterns into CLO3D and then opening them in Marvelous is to simply draw the patterns in Marvelous in the first place.

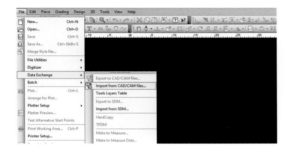

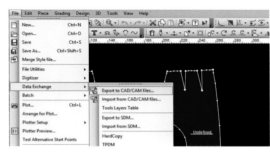

1 Open PDS and go to File > Data Exchange > Import from CAD/CAM Files.

2 From the Import dialogue, select the DXF file format and open the file we just exported from Illustrator.

3 The patterns will appear in the PDS 2D view. Now go to File > Data Exchange > Export to CAD/CAM Files.

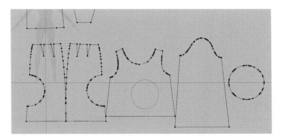

4 Under Format, select AAMA. In the next dialogue, select All Pieces in the File and hit OK.

5 Now that our DXF has been converted to an AAMA, we can open CLO3D. Go to File > Import > DXF > Open. In the Import DXF dialogue, select mm and hit OK, although the patterns have not been made to scale, and therefore will not import to scale.

6 The patterns now appear in the 2D view. Although they are the wrong size, we will simply export them as they are and resize them in Marvelous Designer later. Go to File > Save As > Project and save a project file, which can be opened in Marvelous Designer.

Creating a design with Marvelous Designer

In the following tutorial, we will use the DXF-AAMA files that we previously exported and converted, as the basis for our patterns. We will import and adjust the patterns in Marvelous Designer, place them on the mannequin we previously created in Daz, sew them together and drape them on the model, while adjusting the fabric parameters to suit our needs. The tutorials can be downloaded from the website listed in Resources (page 173).

Marvelous Designer interface

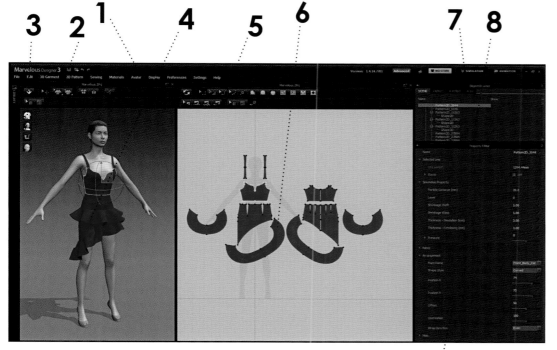

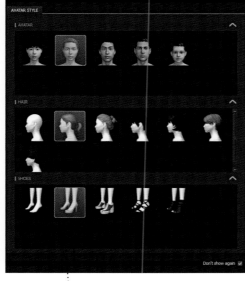

1 Main menu – This is where all of the commands can be found, separated into categories.

2 3D toolbar – This toolbar contains tools that carry out 3D functions.

3 3D view toolbar – The most common 3D tools are represented as icons in this toolbar.

4 3D view – This is where 3D mannequins and garments are displayed.

5 2D view toolbar - The most common 2D tools are represented as icons in this toolbar.

6 Working area – This is the main working area for garment patterns.

7 Simulation/animation interface switch – This switches between the simulation and animation portions of the interface.

8 Scene hierarchy view (in object browser) - This offers a hierarchy of the scene so that objects can be viewed by name.

9 Property editor – This panel displays the properties of the selected objects.

10 Fabric view (in object browser) – This is where fabrics are constructed.

11 Avatar editor – This editor offers avatar options such as body shape, hair and shoes.

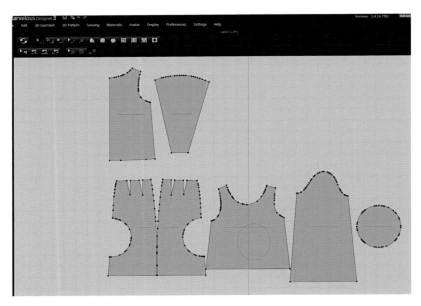

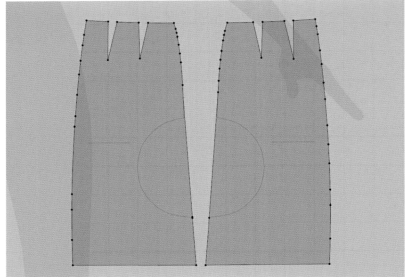

1 In Marvelous Designer now, go to File > Open > Project, and open the project we just saved in Clo3D. The patterns will appear in the 2D view. Drag a selection around all of them with the Transform Pattern tool and scale them down to be around the size of the mannequin.

2 Right-click on the top decoration shape and select Copy; repeat and select Mirror Paste. Move cursor to the right and place the mirrored piece. Repeat for the top back piece. Copy the front and back right pieces of the skirt and duplicate. Select and delete the points on the circle to create straight lines for the side seam.

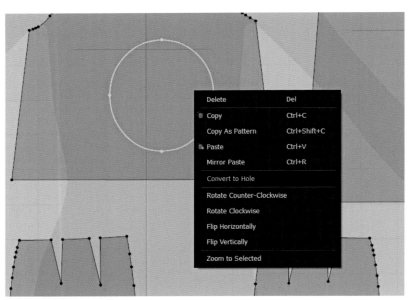

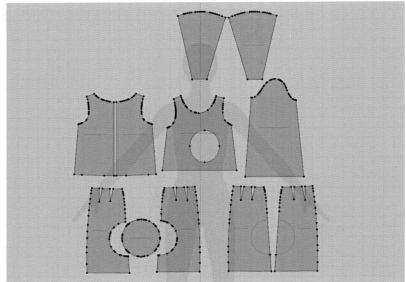

3 Now right-click on the circular internal shape in the middle of the top front and select Convert to Hole from the pop-up menu.

4 This is the complete collection of pieces.

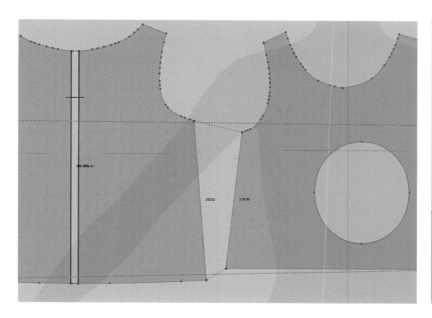

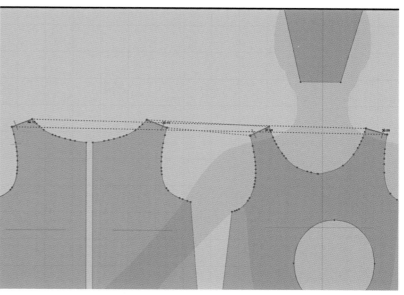

5 We can now start sewing. First, do the sides and centre back with the Segment Sewing tool.

6 Next, sew the shoulder seams bearing in mind that the back pieces will be flipped over in the 3D view.

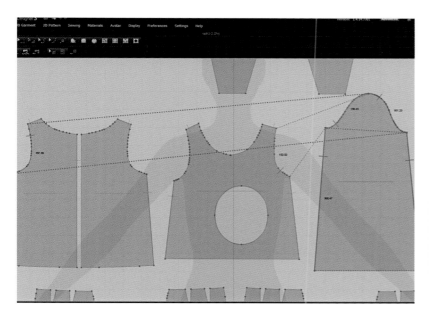

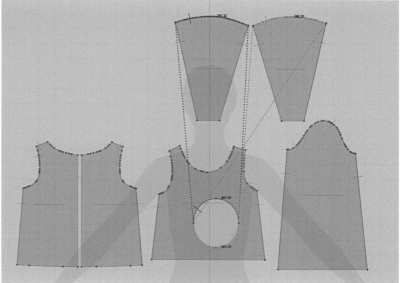

7 Connect the left part of the base of the sleeve to the left sleeve hole of the front piece and the right part to the left sleeve hole (right as it is laid out in the 2D view) of the back piece. Also sew together the sides of the sleeve.

8 Connect the base of the top piece of the decoration to the top half of the hole in the front piece. Do the same for the bottom piece.

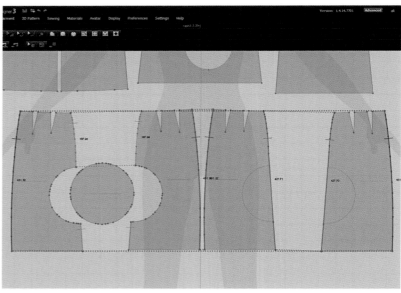

9 Now connect the sides of the pieces.

10 Now use the Free Sewing tool to sew together the sides of the skirt pieces. The Free Sewing tool allows you to sew together any two lengths of edges disregarding edge points, contrary to the Segment Sewing tool, which only works with segments between points.

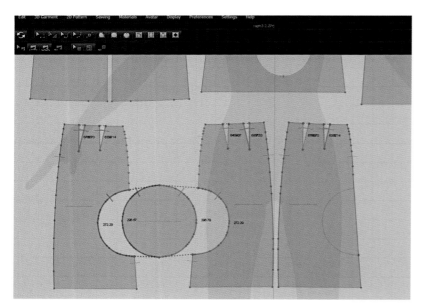

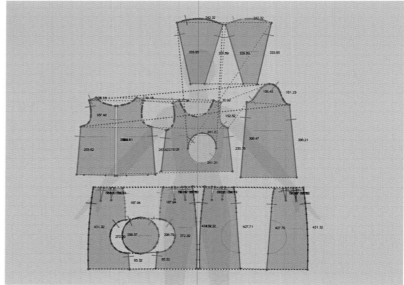

11 Sew the circular decoration shape to the depressions in the skirt pieces with the Free Sewing tool, and the darts with the Segment sewing tool.

12 Here are all the seams.

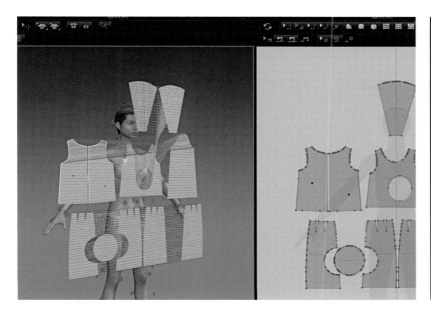

13 Now it's time to place the patterns on the avatar for the 3D draping. Press the Synch button to synchronize the 3D view with the 2D view.

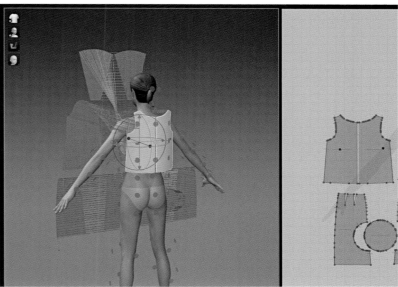

14 Turn on the arrangement points on the avatar by hovering on the small avatar icon near the top left corner of the 2D view and selecting Show Arrangement Points from the extended menu.

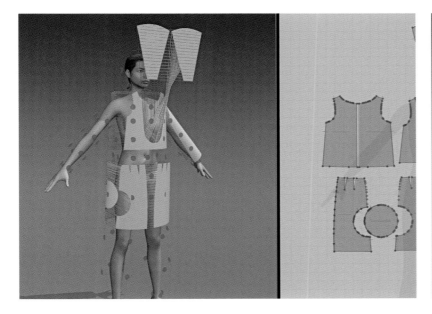

15 Select the two back top pieces (the second one while holding SHIFT), rotate the 3D view (right-click and drag) to see the back of the avatar, and click on arrangement point on the back of the avatar to position the two pieces.

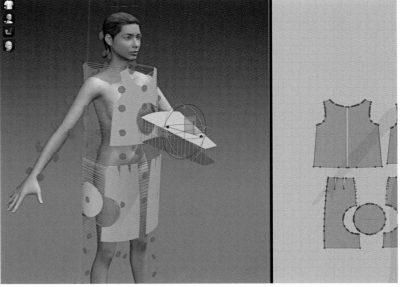

16 Position the other pieces in the same way. From the Preferences menu, select Gizmo > World Coordinate. Select the two decorative pieces and position them separately by clicking and dragging the arrows and the round rotation handles.

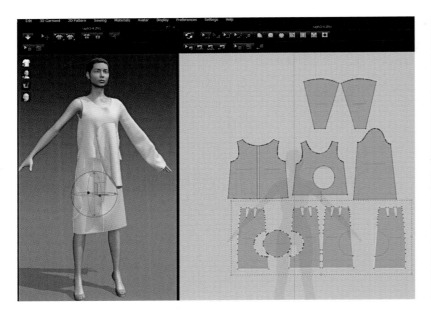

17 Turn off the arrangement points to get a clearer view of the outfit, and hit Play to see it drape. SHIFT-select the patterns in the 2D window, pick up the Transform Pattern tool and scale them up by dragging the corner handles of their collective bounding box.

18 We will now create some of the detailing of the outfit. Start by creating a rectangle with the Create Rectangle Pattern tool, moving the points to taper it slightly with the Edit Pattern tool, and separating its top edge into three parts by inserting two points with the Add Point tool.

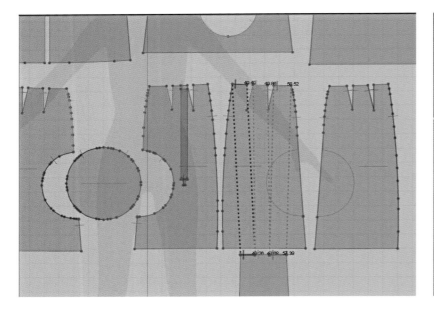

19 The segments should be roughly the same length as the corresponding segments on the top edge of the left front skirt pattern, to which the decorative piece will be sewn. Now sew the two with the Segment Sewing tool.

20 Create a strap using the Create Rectangle Pattern tool, and use the Create Internal Rectangle tool near its base. Right-click on the internal rectangle and select Convert to Hole. Create a rectangle for the metal clip with a line across it using the Internal Line tool (click on one end, SHIFT-double-click on the other).

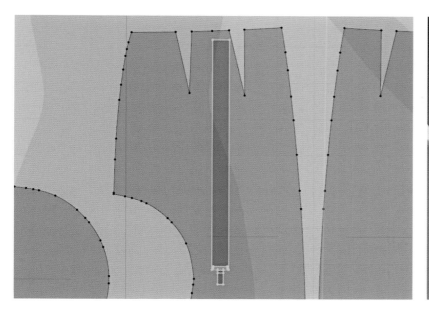

21 Follow the same process to create a second, longer strap for the skirt.

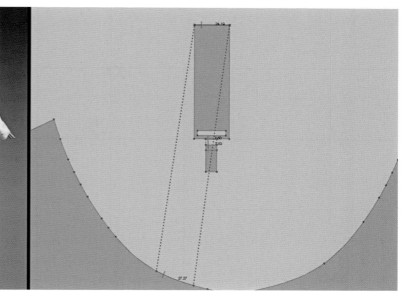

22 Sew the top of the short strap to the neck line with the Free Sewing tool.

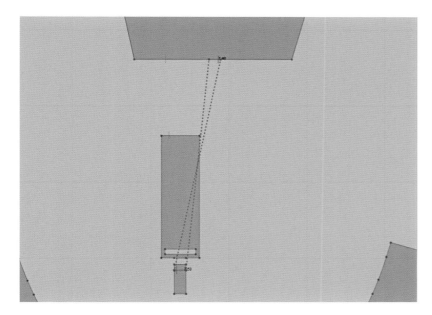

23 Sew the internal line of the clip to the bottom of the sleeve-like decoration. Make sure that the seam is reversed.

24 Sew the long strap on the top of the right front skirt pattern.

25 Create a thin waistband and clip, and an internal line at the other end.

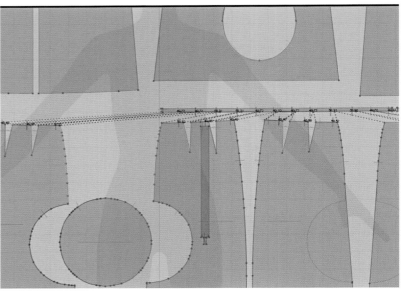

26 With the Free Sewing tool, sew the consecutive segments of the top of the skirt with the bottom edge of the waistband. Make sure that the length of the waistband is roughly the same as the circumference of the skirt.

27 Connect the clip to the waistband, and the internal line to the other end of the waistband.

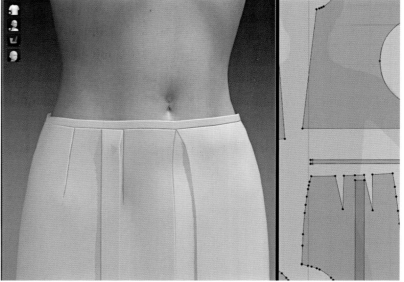

28 Synch the 3D view, position the waistband and run the simulation again.

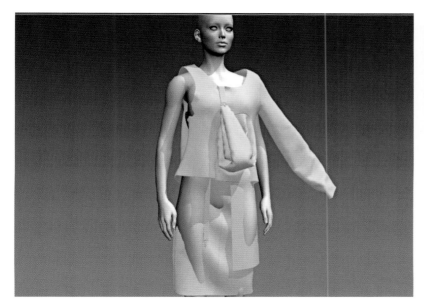

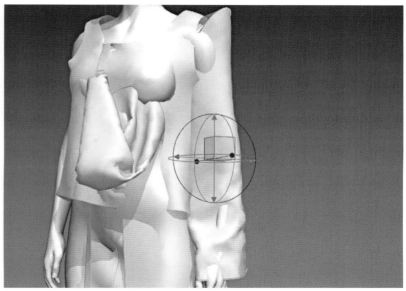

29 It is now time to import our own mannequin. Go to File > Import > Collada. In the Load COLLADA dialogue, select Load as Avatar. As imported avatars do not have arrangement points, it is good practice to work with the default Marvelous avatars and import custom avatars when the majority of the work is done.

30 Move the pieces with the world coordinate gizmo to fit them to the new avatar. Run the simulation again, and pull the garments in the 3D view to help them drape around the avatar. As the garment particles are sparse at 20mm, the cloth will pass through the mannequin surface if pulled strongly enough.

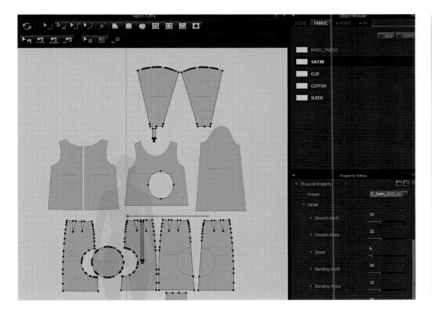

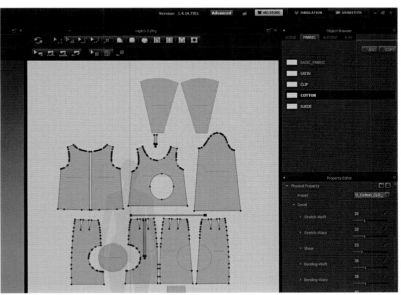

31 In the Fabric section of the Object Browser, click Add to add a new fabric, name it Satin in the Property Editor, and select the Satin preset in the Physical Property section. Drag the fabric from the Object Browser to the patterns.

32 Create a fabric for the clips (use Leather Belt preset) and apply. Then create a cotton fabric (Cotton preset) and apply it to the large decorative pieces.

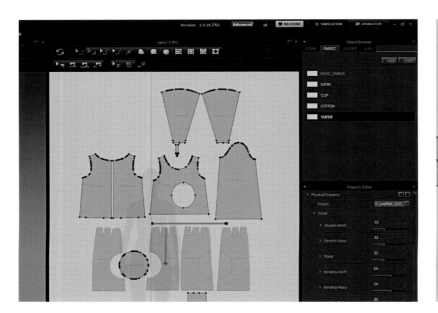

33 Finally, create a suede fabric (leather preset) and apply it to the skirt.

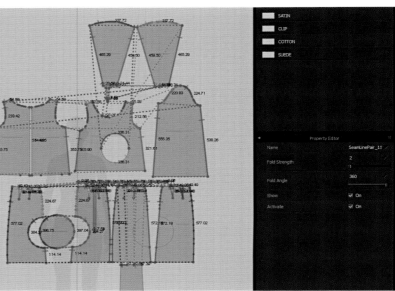

34 With the materials done, drag-select all of the seams with the Edit Seam tool, and in the Property Editor, set the Fold Strength to 2, and the Fold Angle to 360. We are doing this so that our seams will be more prominent on the final design.

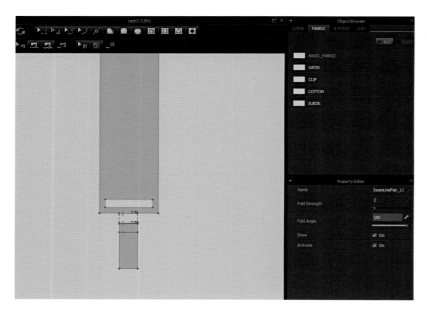

35 Select the seams between clips and straps and change the Fold Angle to 180 so that the clips do not turn outwards.

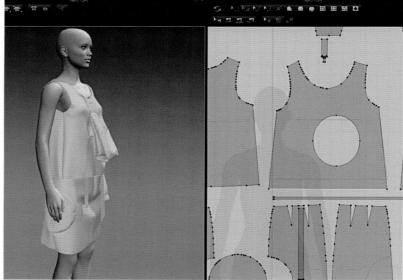

36 Run the simulation again. The design is now very close to the reference, except the front of the top is too short. In the 2D view, select the bottom edge of the top front pattern and drag it down so that the sides of the front and back are about the same.

Exporting for rendering

Animation sequences can also be exported from Marvelous Designer, so that they can be batch-rendered in Maya or another package. This is a very common requirement in film, video game cut-scenes, advertisements, and increasingly in fashion film. The garments are exported from Marvelous Designer as static OBJ models accompanied by a cache file, which describes the movement of the garment through time. Both are then loaded in the destination package (in our case Maya) and the moving garments can be worked on further. The mannequin that was imported into Marvelous Designer is not exported with the garments through this technique; instead, the same mannequin must be separately imported into Maya. The combination of mannequin and clothes is finally shaded and blended with live footage, a 3D scenery, or simply rendered on its own.

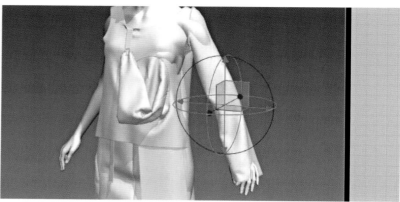

1 We will now import an animated avatar so that we can simulate the design over the period of an entire animation. Go to File > Import > Collada. Select Load as Avatar.

2 Select all the patterns and reposition them on the avatar. Select individual pieces if needed and place them accordingly. Play the simulation and drag the clothes in the 3D view to improve the draping.

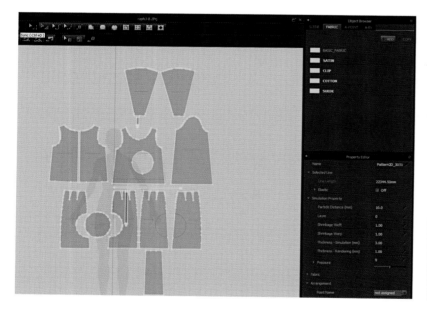

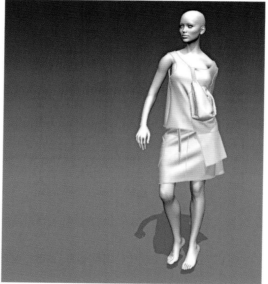

3 Select all the patterns, and in the Property Editor, under Simulation Property, change the Particle Distance to 10mm to increase the resolution (and therefore smoothness) of the clothes. Hit the Sync button to update the 3D view and play the simulation for a few seconds to update it to the new resolution.

4 Go over to the Animation side of the programme, and set the Simulation Quality to Complete. Press Record and observe the design drape over the movement of the avatar. Once the draping is finished, go to File > Save As > Project to save the Marvelous project for later use. Now go to File > Export > Maya Cache to export the design and its animation for use in Autodesk Maya. In the Export Maya Cache dialogue, select Multiple Objects (so that multiple materials can be applied in Maya), Unified UV coordinates (so that our material textures are all the same size), cm for units, and hit OK.

Shading the garments

Once the garments have been created, different materials can be applied to them. Fabrics can be created and applied in the destination 3D package (in our case Blender or Maya); this is usually the preferred method, as it is much more flexible, and it offers much more control over the final render outcome. However, for quick visualization purposes, shading within Marvelous Designer can be very useful. In this case, visual attributes, such as colour, patterns, prints, shine and transparency, are given to each part of the garment. It is quite easy to apply materials to garment parts through a drag-and-drop method, including visual and physical qualities, and to tweak their final appearance in order to get the desired outcome. A 3D-view capture can then be exported as a still image.

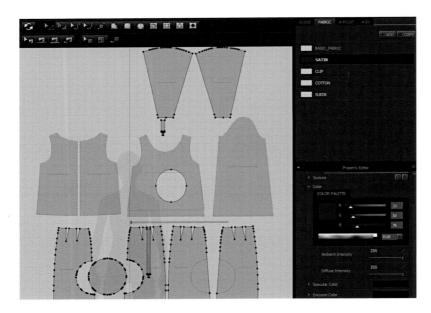

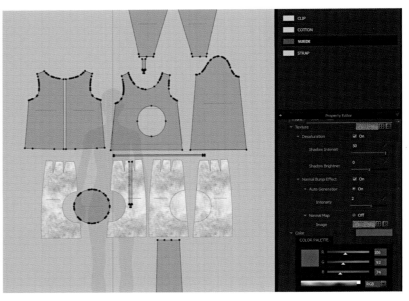

1 In the fabrics panel, click Add to create a new fabric, select the top pieces in the 2D pattern view, and drag and drop the fabric on the pieces. In Property Editor, name the fabric 'Satin', select dark blue in the colour palette under 'Material', and make the specular colour white. Choose satin from the Physical Property presets.

2 Make a new 'Suede' fabric and apply it to the skirt pieces. In the Texture section, click on the small button with four rectangles on it, and load a suede texture. Turn on Normal Bump Effect and Auto Generation; also, turn up the Intensity to 2. Turn Desaturation on, and tint the texture with the Color Palette in the Color Section.

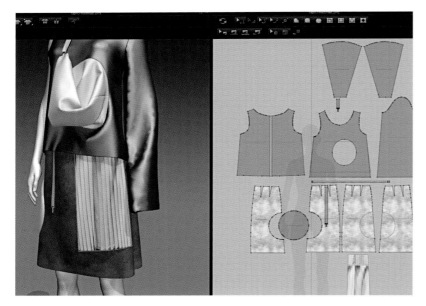

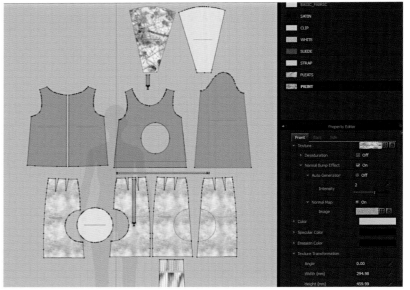

3 Repeat step 2 for the pleated piece of fabric on the front of the skirt. Adjust the Color and Texture Transformations options so that the colour of the fabric is a bluish grey and so the pleats texture fits the pattern rectangle perfectly and does not repeat/wrap.

4 Make another fabric for the white side of the decorative 'sleeve'. Make it an off-white colour, and add a normal map for the weave texture. Make a similar fabric for the patterned side of the 'sleeve', but this time also give it a colour texture.

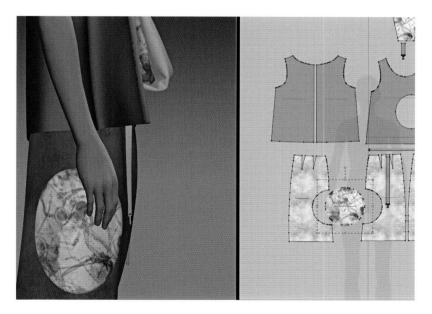

5 Make one more fabric like the last, and apply it to the circular decorative piece on the skirt.

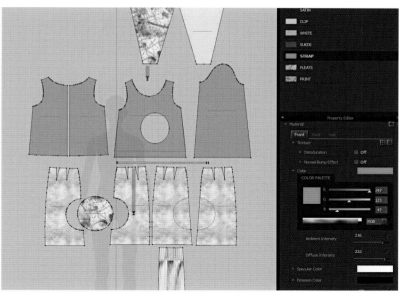

6 Make a shiny (white specular colour) orange fabric for the straps and apply it.

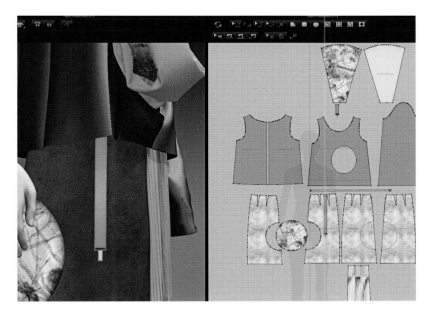

7 Similarly, make a shiny grey material for the strap clips and apply it.

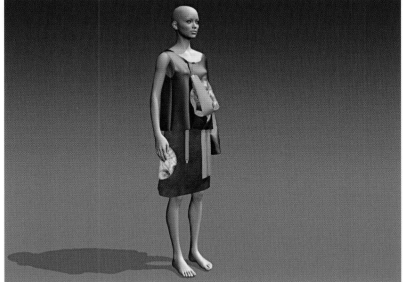

8 This is the complete shaded outfit.

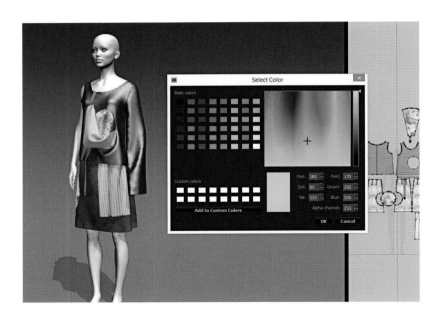

9 To change the background, go to Preferences > 3D Background Color and select a colour from the colour picker palette. Also, under Display, turn the Show Background Image option off, for the colour to show.

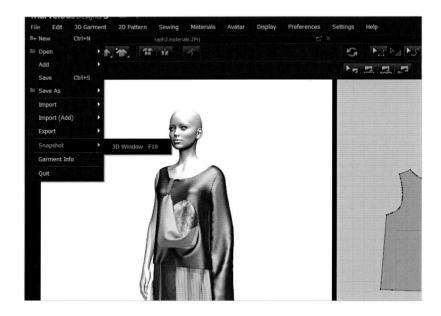

10 To save a snapshot of the 3D view, go to File > Snapshot > 3D Window, and save the file as a PNG image.

Creating a garment with V-Stitcher

Constructing an Anne Valerie Hash garment

V-Stitcher is an industrial fashion CAD program made by a company called Browzwear. Its features are similar to those of CLO3D (and Marvelous Designer), as well as the Optitex and Lectra solutions. In the following tutorial, I will use a design by fashion designer Anne Valerie Hash. The patterns will be imported, manipulated and placed on a 3D mannequin. Cloth simulation will then allow us to drape the garment on the model and adjust it, until the desired outcome is achieved.

V-Stitcher interface

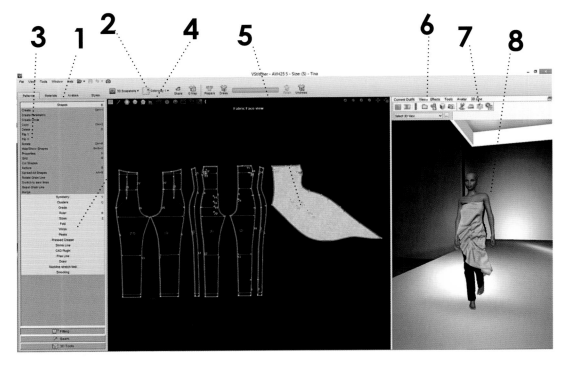

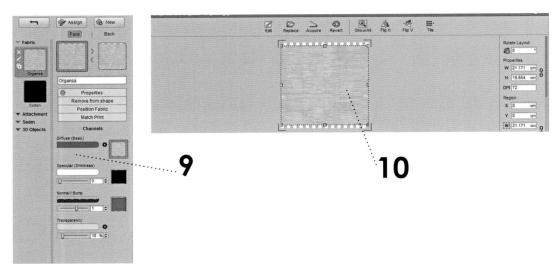

1 Main menu – This is where all of the commands can be found, separated into categories.

2 Main icons bar– The most common tools are represented as icons in this toolbar.

3 Panel tabs – These tabs open up different panels.

4 Main toolbox – The most common tools are represented as icons in this toolbar.

5 Working area – This is the main working area for garment patterns.

6 3D menu – This menu contains commands that apply in the 3D window.

7 3D toolbar – This toolbar contains tools that carry out 3D functions.

8 3D view – This is where 3D mannequins and garments are displayed.

9 Materials panel – This is where fabrics are created.

10 Image editor – This is the area for the loading and editing of image.

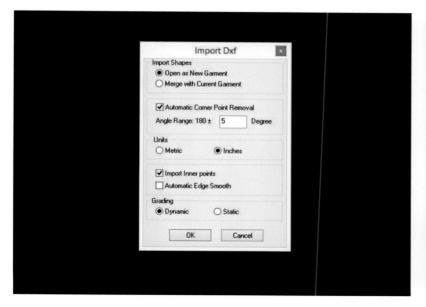

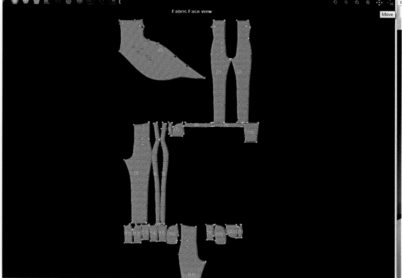

1 Go to File > Import and from the Import DXF dialogue, select Open As New Garment, Inches, and Import Inner Points. There is no grading involved so leave the default option on. Choose X1 as size factor.

2 In the Garment Map window, select the type of garment ('overall'), and the name (AVH25). As we are only constructing one garment and there is no grading, this dialogue does not matter too much.

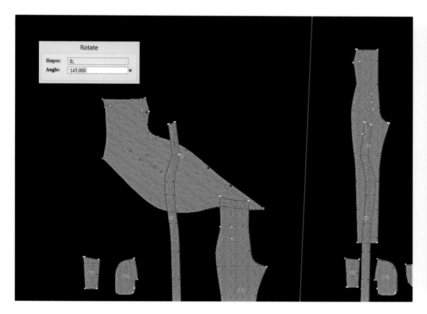

3 Now rotate the pieces so they are upright. In the Patterns tab on the left, under Shapes, click Rotate. Drag-select all the pieces, and in the Rotate dialogue, type in 90 for the rotation angle. The front organza piece is cut on the bias, so rotate it 145 degrees.

4 Lay out all the pieces using the Move tool.

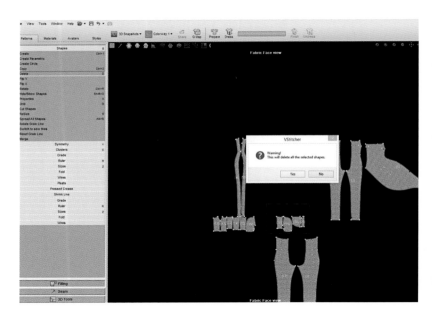

5 Select the Delete option under Patterns > Shapes, and select to delete any pieces that are not needed, such as lining.

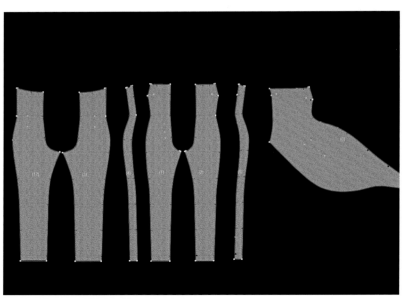

6 These are the pieces I kept to put together the garment.

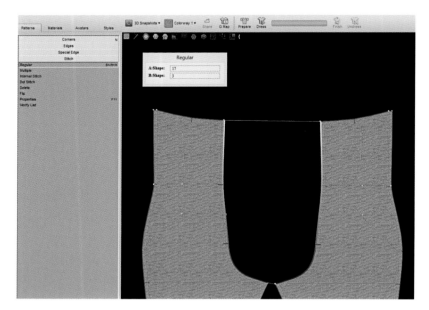

7 To stitch the pieces together, go to the Stitch section of Patterns and select Regular. Click on the centre seam of the left back piece, then on the centre seam of the opposite piece.

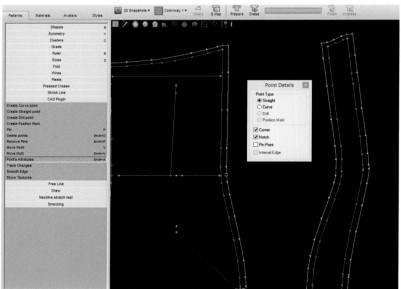

8 Under Patterns> CAD Plugin, select Create Curve Point and click on the pattern edge to add a point, or Delete Point and click delete. To find out what kind a point is, select Point's Attributes and then the point in question. You can convert the point from the same dialogue ('corner points' act as ends of seams).

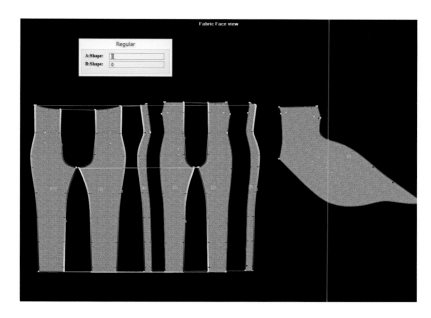

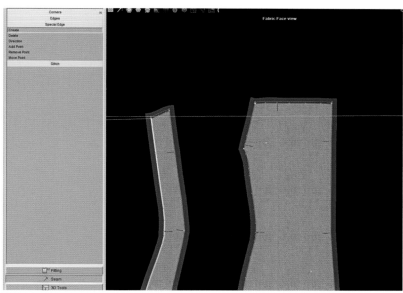

9 Sew all the pieces together, as in the illustration, making sure to sew the inside of the front right leg to the inside of the inside of the back left leg, and vice versa.

10 Now go to Patterns > Edges > Allowance, select all the pieces, and set 1cm for the allowance.

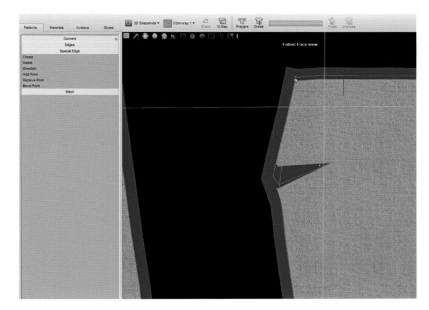

11 We must now create an edge inside the darts so that we can sew their sides together. Go to Patterns > Seam > Special Edge > Create, and click clockwise, from dart edge point, to dart inside point, to the other edge point. Right-click to confirm.

12 Sew the side of the organza piece to the side seam of the overall with the Regular Stitch tool. Then use the Stitch > Flip tool to flip it – some seams are created the wrong way around due to the direction of the edge and the Flip tool helps amend this.

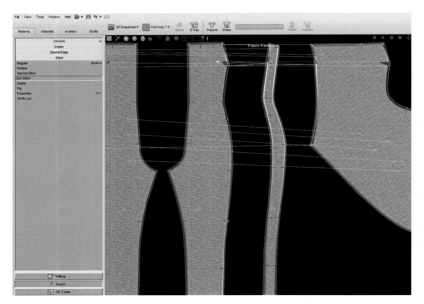

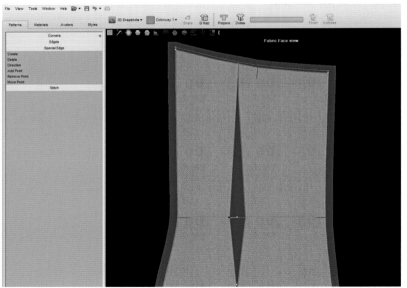

13 Use the Dot Stitch tool to sew points on the organza piece to the main patterns. These are used for the draping effect of the organza decoration.

14 Turn the textures off so you can see the points on the blocks more easily, and go to Patterns > Special Edge > Create. Click on the points as shown from to top to bottom, then from the bottom of the dart up to the very top, clockwise. This will create a dart whose edges can be stitched together; next, stitch the seams.

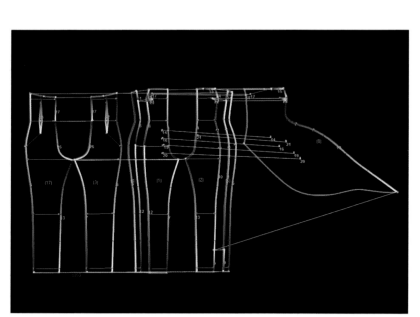

15 This is the garment with all seams applied.

16 To start placing the pieces in the 3D view, go to Patterns > Clusters > New. Drag a box around each cluster of patterns as in the illustration. With the Move tool, push the pieces closer to overlap slightly, so placement on the mannequin will be easier.

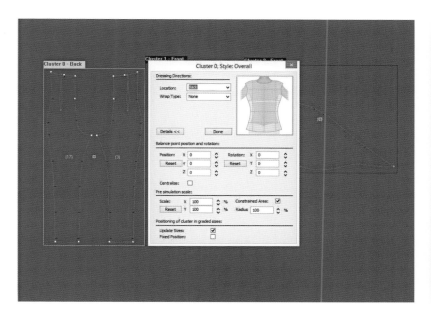

17 With the Cluster > Edit tool, select the clusters and set their location around the mannequin (back, front and front).

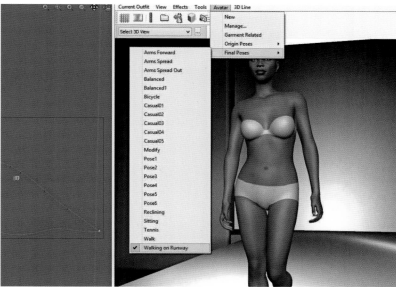

18 In the 3D window, go to Avatar > Origin Poses > Hands at 90, and then to Final Poses > Walking on Runway. The original pose allows us to place the clusters on the mannequin, and the final pose of the mannequin allows the garment to drape around a specific pose.

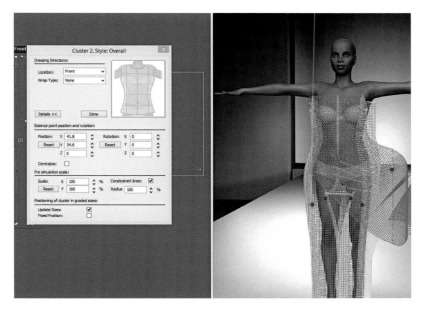

19 Click the Prepare icon so that the clusters appear in the 3D view. Control-click and drag the clusters on the mannequin to position them better. Left-click and drag to orbit the view around the mannequin, and refine the positions of the rest of the clusters.

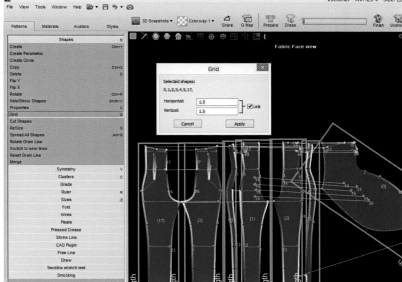

20 We will now change the resolution of the pieces for more accurate simulation. Go to Shapes > Grid, select all pieces and change both vertical and horizontal distances to 1.5.

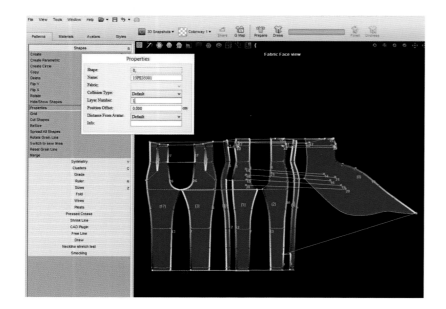

21 Then, with Shapes > Properties change the Layer Number of the front organza piece to 1 so that it simulates on top of the other pieces, which are on layer 0.

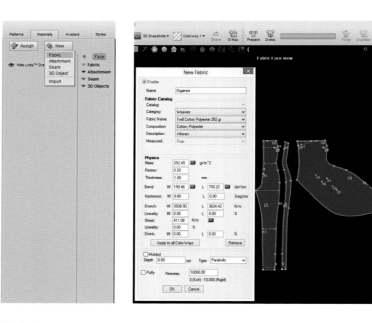

22 Time to apply materials. Go over to the Material tab, click the New button and select Fabric. In the New Fabric window, select a fabric from the presets and confirm.

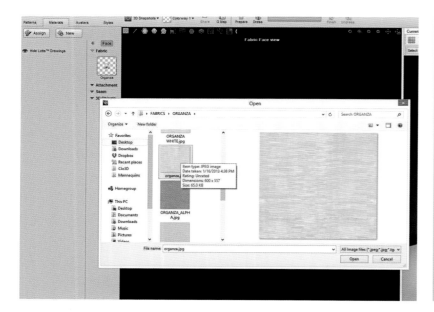

23 Next, click on the Fabric Face icon and select an organza texture.

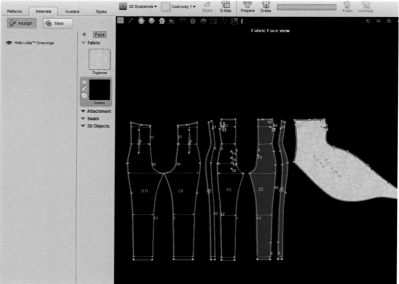

24 Click the Assign button, and assign the new fabric to the organza piece. Repeat the process for the main black cotton fabric and apply it to the rest of the pieces.

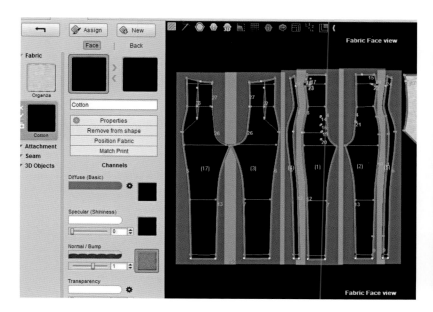

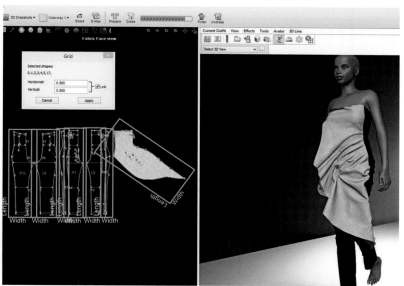

25 Click on the Edit icon next to the fabric textures to go to the full fabric interface. Select a specular (shine) and a normal (bumps) map for the organza, and turn the transparency up to 10%. Load specular and normal maps for the main fabric as well.

26 Set the grid of the patterns to 0.5 (Shapes > Grid), and run the simulation (Dress button). This will increase the resolution of the simulation and improve its quality.

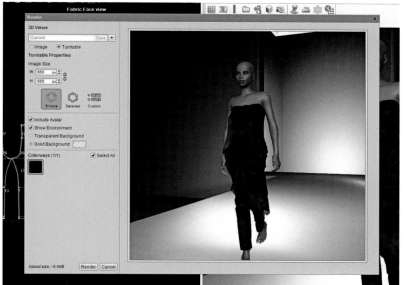

27 Go to File > Export and select Browzwear 3D Object as the format. In the Export 3D Objects dialogue, select both avatar and garment. The outcome will be viewed on the standalone BWO Viewer in 3D.

29 Go to File > Export, choose the Turntable (.html) format to render 2D images from all angles so that the model can be displayed on Internet browsers. To export as a 3D object, use the .obj or the .fbx format; select the default options in the options dialogue.

Creating a garment with Optitex and Blender

Constructing a Boudicca dress

PDS is a piece of software by fashion CAD company Optitex. It has similar features to V-Stitcher and CLO3D/Marvelous Designer, and as it has been around for many years, it is preferred by many fashion companies and colleges. In the following tutorial, I will import the patterns of a dress by British fashion house Boudicca, and I will follow a similar process to the previous tutorials. The patterns will be sewn together, the fabrics will be adjusted based on real-world physics attributes, the pieces will be placed on a 3D fashion model, and the dress will finally be draped. The dress will finally be imported into Blender, an open-source but extremely versatile 3D software, and rendered using Blender's physically accurate Cycles renderer.

Optitex interface

1   2   3   4   5   6   7

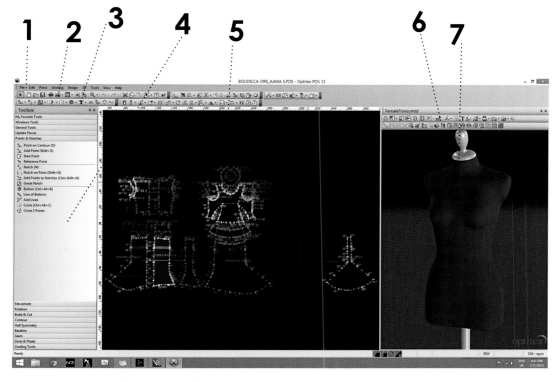

1 Main menu - This is where all of the commands can be found, separated into categories.

2 Main toolbar – The most common tools are represented as icons in this toolbar.

3 Icon toolbars – These are toolbars with various sets of tools.

4 TThe Toolbox – This contains tools for pattern drafting and updating, divided into groups according to their functionality.

5 Working Area – This is the main working area for garment patterns.

6 3D toolbars – Contains tools that carry out 3D functions.

7 3D viewport – This is where 3D mannequins and garments are displayed.

8 3D properties panel – Offers information on 3D pieces and allows their manipulation.

9 Pieces panel – Offers the list of pieces in the working area in the form of icons.

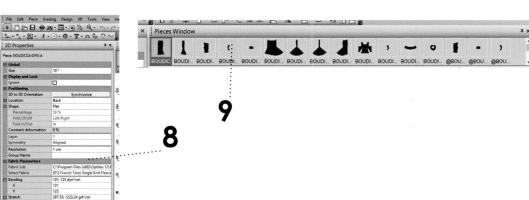

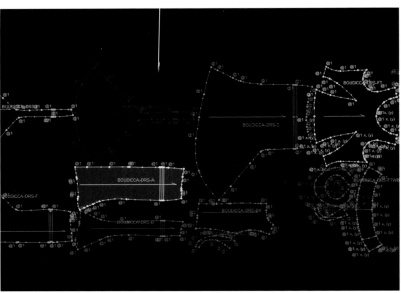

1 We'll load our patterns by going to File > Data Exchange > Import from CAD/CAM files. In the dialogue, browse for the file, select cm and AAMA, and confirm. The patterns will appear on top of one another.

2 To lay them out, go to File > Arrange for Plot, select All Pieces in File – I also chose 110 for Width and 1 for Gap – and confirm. The patterns are now laid out within a rectangle area next to each other.

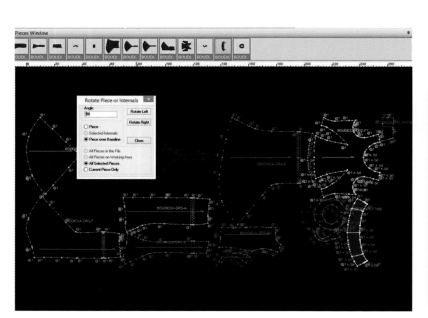

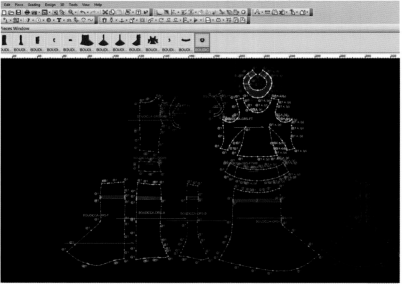

3 Drag-select the pieces and go to Piece > Modify > Rotate. Set the angle to 90 and rotate left.

4 Drag the pieces around with the Move tool to arrange them as shown.

62 Creating garments

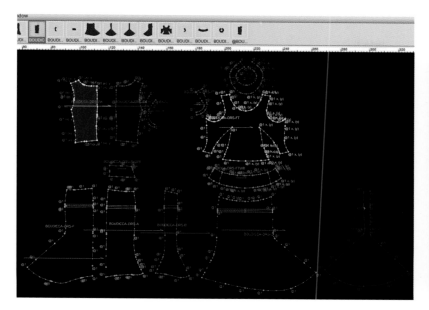

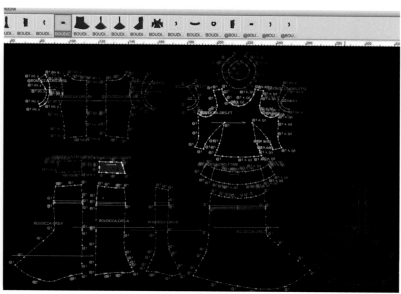

5 Select the top right piece, go to Edit > Copy, Edit > Paste to paste a copy next to the original, and Piece > Modify > Flip Horizontally to flip it over.

6 Do the same for all pieces that are half or only on one side.

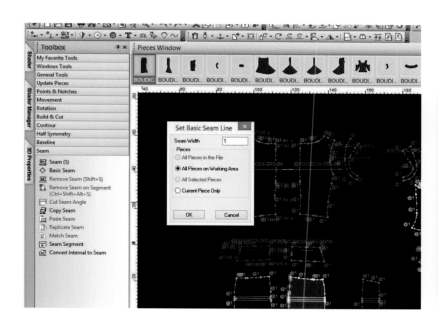

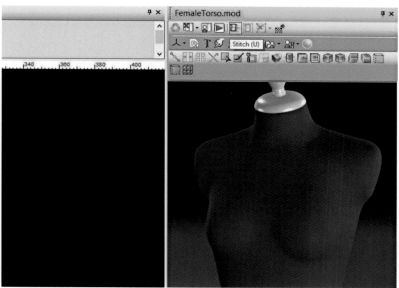

7 In the Toolbox, go to Seam > Basic Seam, set the Width to 1 and select All Pieces on Working Area. This will add a seam allowance of 1cm to all pieces.

8 Go to View > 3D Windows > Model to bring up the 3D view, from which you can pick the Stitch tool.

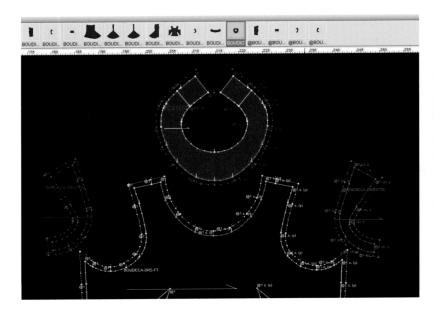

9 Stitch together all the pieces as per the illustrations.

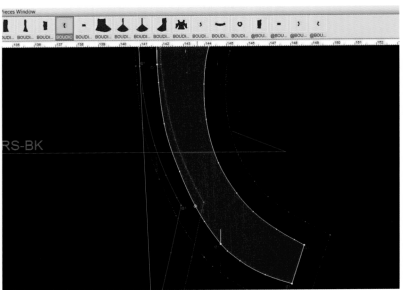

10 Some piece edges will need to be broken down into smaller segments by inserting new points on them. To do this, go to Points and Notches > Point on Contour, and click on an edge to insert a point. The Stitch tool can then be used to stitch the edge up to the newly introduced point.

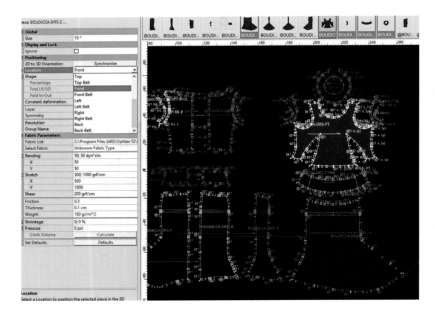

11 In the 3D Properties Window (which can be opened through the View > 3D Windows menu), select each piece and set its location on the mannequin in the Positioning section.

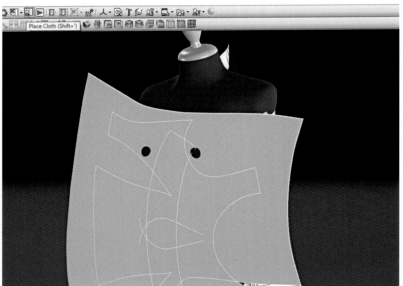

12 When all pieces are roughly located, click the Place Cloth icon in the 3D view to bring the patterns over to this view.

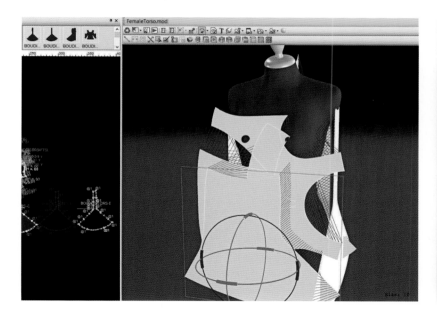

13 From the 3D Transform icon, select 3D Rotate Piece, and select and rotate the pieces that face the wrong way by dragging on the differently coloured handles of the tool.

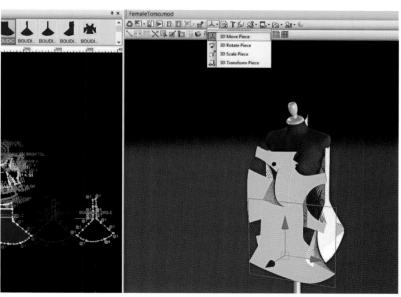

14 To move the pieces around, use the 3D Move Piece from the same menu.

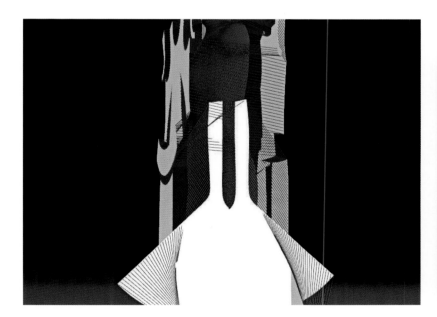

15 Move and rotate the pieces to place them appropriately around the mannequin, as per the illustrations.

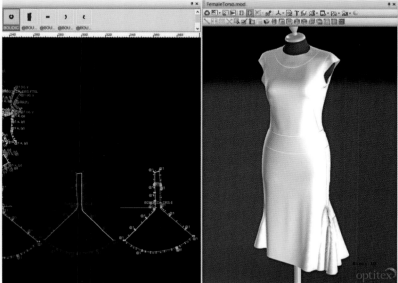

16 With all the pieces sewn and placed, we can now run the simulation. Click on the Simulate Draping (Play) icon.

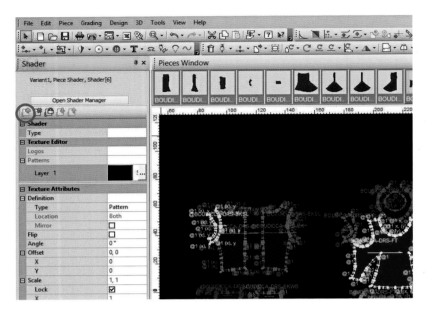

17 Select all of the pieces in the 2D view, and in the Shader menu (available in the View menu) click on the Add Layer menu. In the Texture Editor, next to Layer 1, load a fabric texture and adjust the scale of the texture as well as the shine of the material.

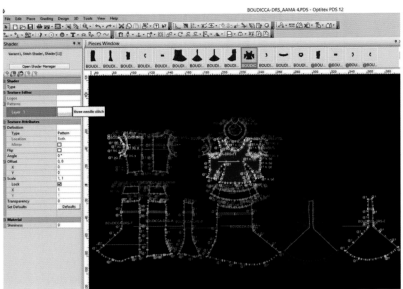

18 For the appearance of the seams, click on the Show Stitch Mode icon in the 3D view and select all the seams in the 2D view. Then in the Shader palette, next to Layer 1, select the Three Needle Stitch, or another seam texture preset.

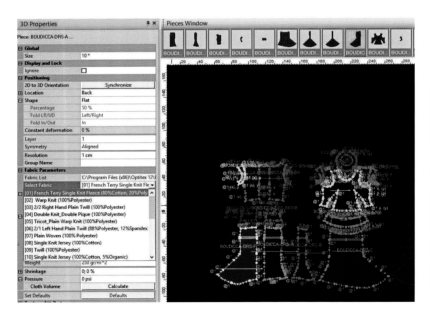

19 Select all of the patterns, open the 3D Properties panel once more, and under Fabric Parameters, select a fabric preset. Run the simulation again.

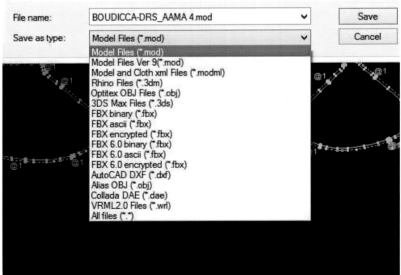

20 There are various ways to save designs from Optitex. A convenient option is Model Files (.mod) in the 3D view Save icon, under the Save Model choice, which allows the view of a design in Optitex's own standalone 3D viewer.

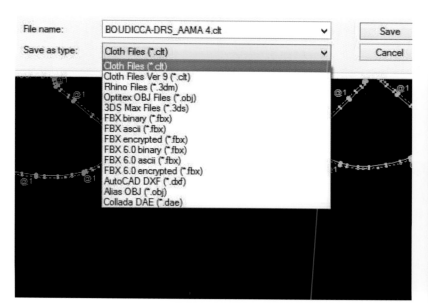

21 Under the same menu, Save Cloth will allow you to save only the garments for viewing in the same 3D viewer.

22 Yet another option in the same menu is Snapshot, which exports a 2D image of the perspective or of four views. This can be any resolution and .jpeg or .png format.

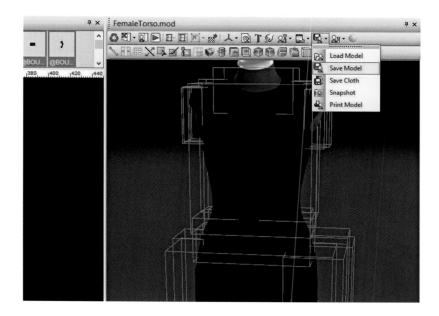

23 Finally, the model can be exported as 3D geometry for use in another package through the Save Model > .obj option. File > Save As will save the whole file for further work in Optitex.

Blender interface

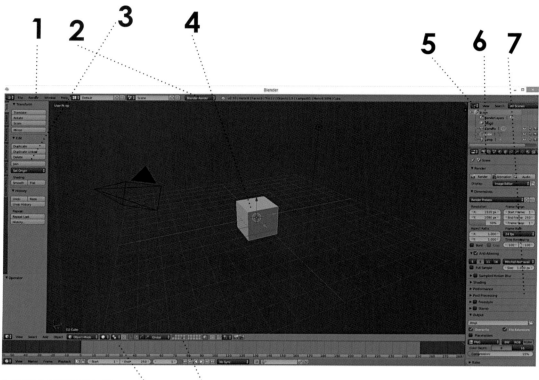

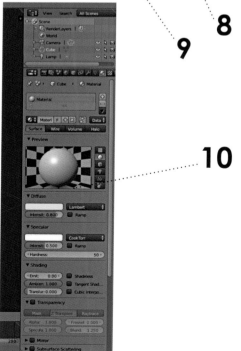

1 Main menu – This is where all of the commands can be found, separated into categories.

2 Renderer selection menu – This menu selects the current renderer.

3 Object tools panel – This panel offers tools for the manipulation of 3D objects.

4 3D viewport – This is where the 3D scenes are navigated and manipulated.

5 Scene hierarchy editor – This offers a hierarchy of the scene so that objects can be selected by name.

6 Editor tab icons – These icons open up different panels.

7 Render editor – This is where interactive rendering (IPR) and final rendering are displayed.

8 Editor menu – Each editor has its own menu of commands.

9 Timeline editor – This defines the playback range and current time of an animation.

10 Materials editor – This is where the materials are created.

1 As the programme opens, the intro screen will appear. Select the interface setup you prefer. I usually prefer the Maya setup, but if you are not familiar with Maya, you may prefer the standard Blender setup. To delete the cube that occupies the new scene, left-click and press [Delete] on the keyboard, then confirm.

2 To load the Optitex model we just created (or any other 3D model), go to File > Import > Wavefront (.obj). Select the file in the browser and click the Import OBJ button in the top right corner. The model then appears in the 3D viewport.

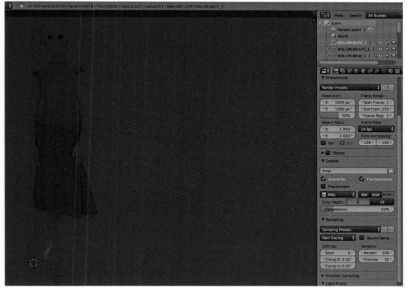

3 The standard Blender renderer is Blender Render. To use the superior Cycles renderer, go to the drop-down menu at the top of the screen and select 'Cycle Render'. Near the bottom of the screen, there is a sphere icon, which defines the viewport shading method. Select 'Material' for a rough representation of materials.

4 In the Render section (camera button) of the editor on the right, you can find all the options that apply to rendering. Change the Render Samples to 1000, and the Preview Samples to 100. Also, under Light Paths, change Integrator Presets to Full Global Illumination. This is the preferred rendering method.

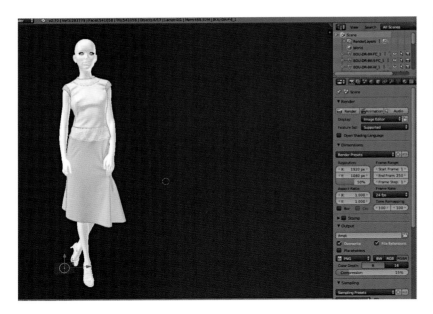

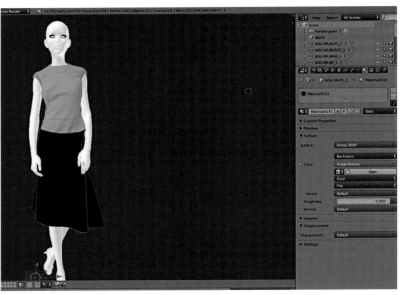

5 Select all of the dress pieces in the 3D viewport by SHIFT-left-clicking. You will need to orbit the view by ALT-left-clicking and dragging in the viewport. In the materials tab (the button with the checkered sphere), in the Surface section, select the Glossy BSDF material preset.

6 Click next to Color and select Image Texture from the pop-up menu. Click on the Open button and select an image file to open. The dress is now textured with an image map.

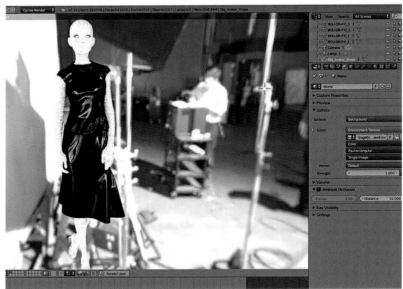

7 Select the pre-assigned model materials that relate to the mannequin and under Surface, apply a subsurface scattering material. We will apply a texture to these as well in a minute, after we have set up the lighting.

8 In the World tab that looks like the Earth, select Background for Surface, and Environment Texture for Color. The Equirectangular option allows the texture to wrap around the scene properly. Click open to load an image and adjust its strength; I set mine to 0.500.

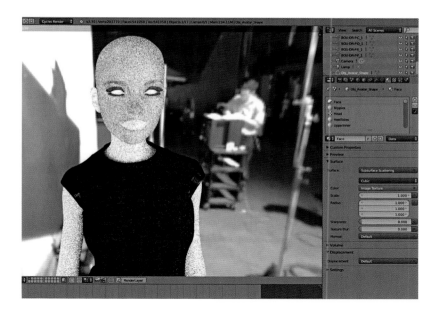

9 Now that the lighting has been set up, we can apply textures to the subsurface scattering material on the mannequin and adjust it. Go over the mannequin materials again and load the appropriate texture images. You may also want to adjust the Roughness and add displacement maps.

10 Finally, go in the Render menu and select Render Image to render the scene into an image file.

Creating accessories and jewellery

Rhino and Octane

So far we have covered a few different software packages for fashion design, but what about accessories? For product design like this, there are other 3D packages that one can use, such as Solidworks, Inventor, 3ds Max, AutoCAD, and Rhino3D. Rhino is one of the most commonly used pieces of software for product design and architecture, but it is equally popular with shoe, accessory, and jewellery designers. In the next two tutorials, we will use Rhino3D to create a leather bag and a ring. The 3D objects will finally be exported and rendered using one of the most physically accurate renderers, Octane.

Rhino interface

1 2 3 4 5 6 7 8

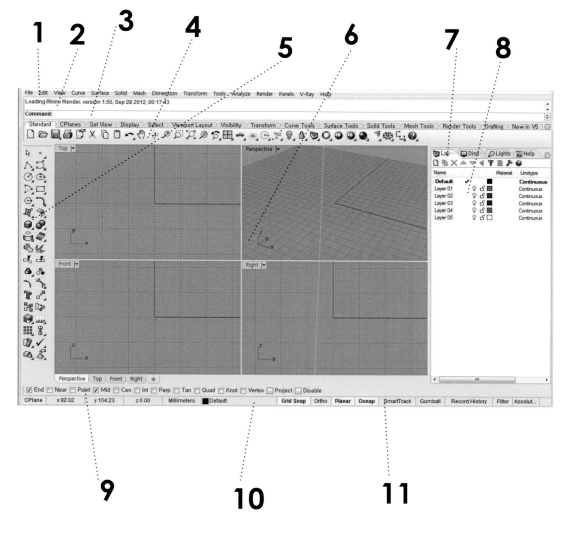

9 10 11

1 Main menu – This is where all of the commands can be found, separated into categories.

2 Command history – This area displays the previous commands carried out.

3 Command prompt – This area displays prompts for the user to carry out commands.

4 Icon toolbars – These are toolbars with various sets of tools.

5 Main toolbar – The most common tools are represented as icons in this toolbar.

6 3D viewports – This is where the 3D scenes are navigated and manipulated.

7 Panel tabs – These tabs open up different panels.

8 Layers panel - This panel shows Display Layers for scene management.

9 Onsnap toolbar – The Onsnap toolbar consists of detailed options for snapping objects together.

10 Layers quick access – A simplified version of the Layers panel.

11 Snap toolbar – The snap toolbar consists of options for snapping objects together.

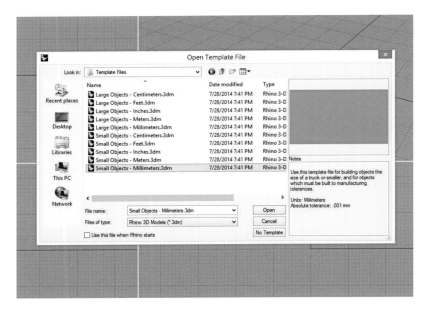

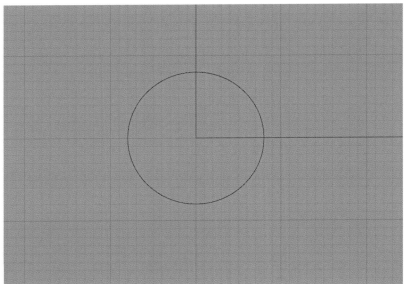

1 Let's create a new document by going to File > New. Rhino will then ask us to choose a template file to load. As we will be working with jewellery, Small Objects – Millimeters seems appropriate. In the front view double click on the view title to maximize it.

2 To draw a circle based on a centre point and radius go to Curve > Circle > Centre, Radius. On the 'Centre of circle' prompt place the centre point at the origin by turning on the Grid Snap option and clicking, or by typing 0,0 in the command line. On the 'Radius' prompt click on the 'Diameter' option, type in 16mm and [Enter].

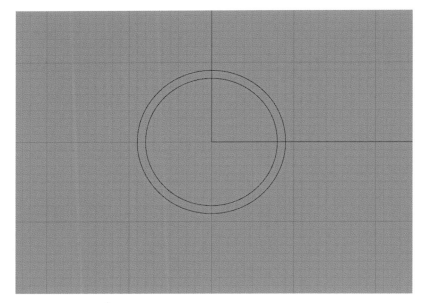

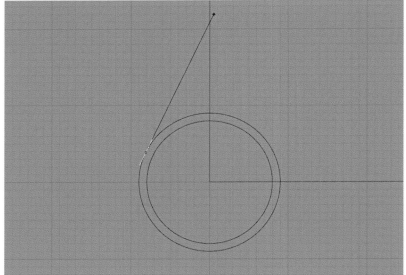

3 Using the same command, create a 18mm circle around the original circle.

4 Next, in the Curve menu, this time select Line > Tangent from Curve. On the 'Start of line' prompt, click on a point on the left of the outside circle just above the horizontal axis. On the 'End of line' prompt, click about 1cm higher and through the vertical axis.

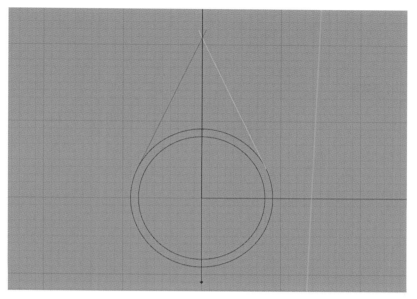

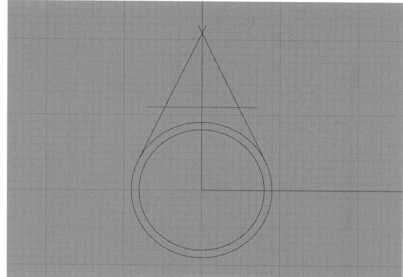

5 We'll now mirror the line by going to Transform > Mirror. On the 'Select objects to mirror' prompt, select the line. On the 'Start of mirror plane' prompt, make sure the 'Copy' option is on, and click anywhere along the vertical (green) axis. On the 'End of mirror plane' prompt, click anywhere else along the vertical axis.

6 Next, we'll create the top line of the ring by going to Curve > Line > Single Line. Click above the circles and to the left of the left diagonal line, then hold [Shift] and click to the right of the right diagonal line. [Shift] by default restricts movement to horizontal, vertical, or 45 degree diagonal.

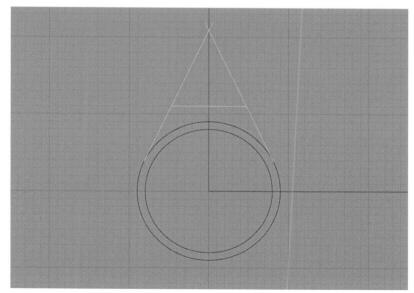

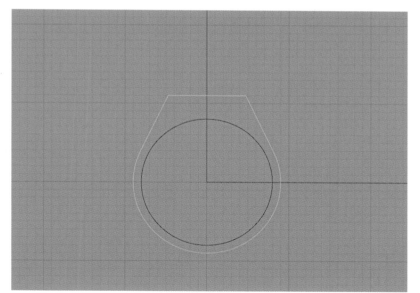

7 We will now use Edit > Trim to trim excess line segments. On the 'Select cutting objects' prompt, select all three lines. On the 'Select objects to trim' prompt, click on excessive line segments to trim. Then click on the top of the outside circle to trim this as well.

8 Our curves are now trimmed but separate so we must use Edit > Join to combine them. Select all of the outside curves and press [Enter] to join them. up the 3D view, from which you can pick the Stitch tool.

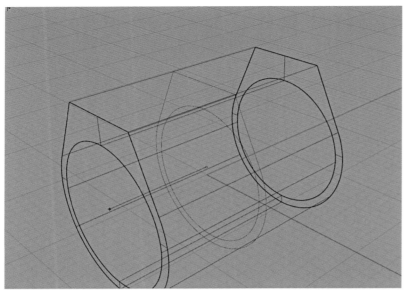

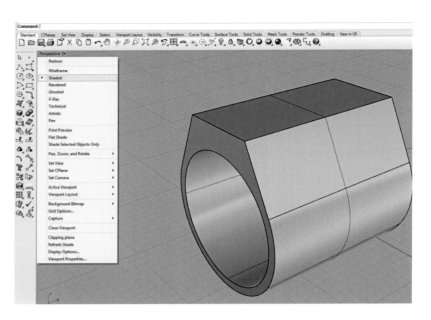

9 To extrude curves to turn them into a 3D solid in the perspective view, go to Solid > Extrude Planar Curve > Straight, and on the 'Select curves to extrude' prompt, select all of the curves. On the 'Extrusion distance' prompt, make sure that the Both Sides and Solid options are set to 'Yes' – click on them if not to turn them on.

10 Type '10' in the command line to create a 10mm thick extrusion on each side, a total of 20cm. Right-click on the perspective view title in the top left corner of the viewport and select the 'Shaded' display.

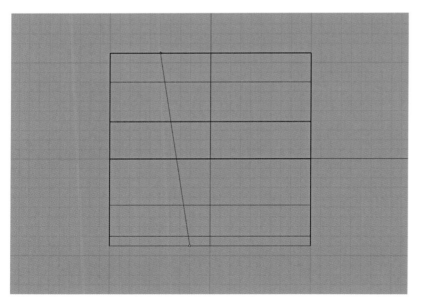

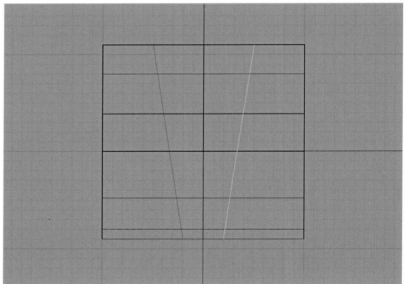

11 In the right view now, the ring currently looks too fat, but we will trim it. Go to Curve > Line > Single Line. Then draw a slightly skewed line from above the top of the ring to below the bottom, intersecting the whole ring.

12 Use Transform > Mirror to mirror copy the line. The start and the end of the mirror plane are both anywhere on the vertical axis.

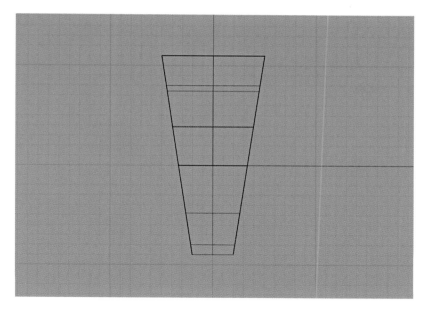

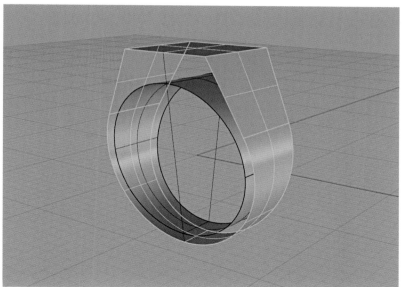

13 Go to Edit > Trim, select the two skewed lines as cutting objects, press [Enter] and then click on the ring parts outside the lines to trim them. Press [Enter] again to finalize.

14 Orbiting the view around the ring in the perspective view, reveals that there are some surfaces missing to close the shape. To fix this, go to Solid > Cap Planar Holes, select the outside polysurface (combined set of surfaces) to cap and press [Enter] to confirm.

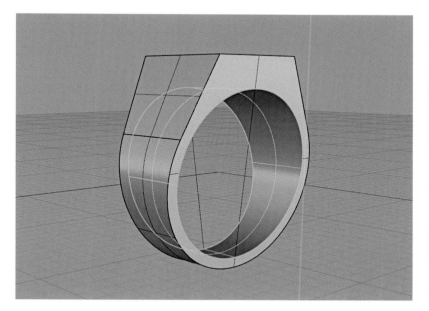

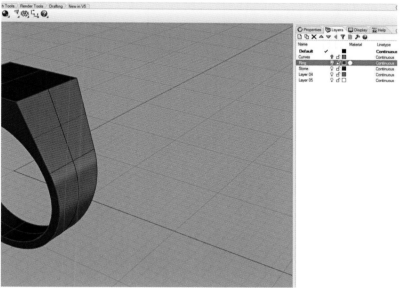

15 This will cover the entire sides, but we will trim the inside surfaces. Use Edit > Trim and on the 'Select cutting objects prompt' select the inside ring surface and confirm. Then select the inside disc areas to trim them. Next it is time for some housekeeping.

16 In Layers, there are five pre-made layers. Right-click on Layer 01 and rename it Curves; select all curves in our scene, right-click on the Curves layer and select Change Object Layer to put all curves in this layer. Then put all ring surfaces in a layer called Ring.

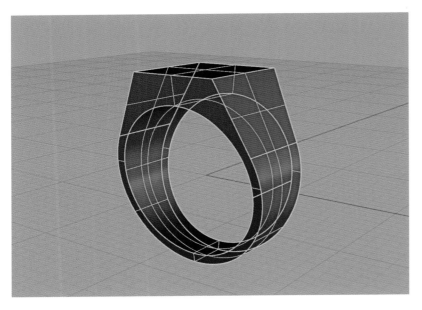

17 Edit > Join all of the ring surfaces together.

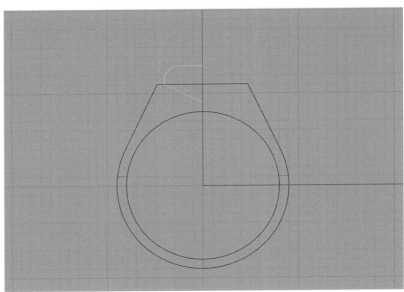

18 We will now start to create the stone for our ring. In the front view, go to Curve > Polyline > Polyline and draw a half diamond shape like the one in the illustration. Having Grid Snap on will help, as you must start and finish the polyline on the vertical axis.

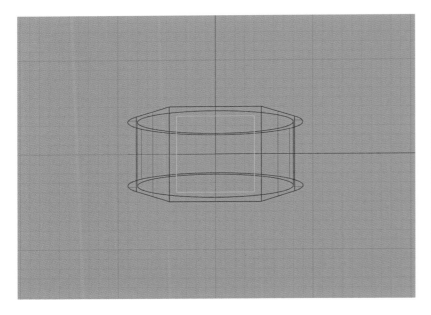

19 In the top view, select the Curve > Rectangle > Corner to Corner command, and draw a rectangle inside the top rectangle of the ring (again, Grid Snap helps) by placing two corner points.

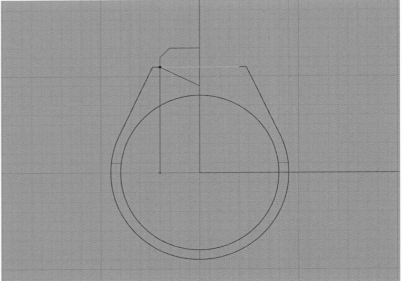

20 This step is not necessary, but it helps understand the process better. Transform > Move the rectangle in the front view from the origin up to the top of the ring.

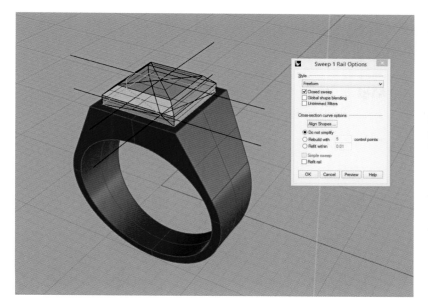

21 To combine the diamond profile curve and the rectangle rail curve to make a diamond solid, go to Surface > Sweep 1 Rail, select the rectangle for a rail and the half-diamond for a cross section. In the Sweep 1 Rail options panel, select 'Freeform', 'Close sweep', and 'Do not simplify', and confirm.

22 Make a new layer and call it 'Stone' (or rename an existing one), and put the stone solid in it.

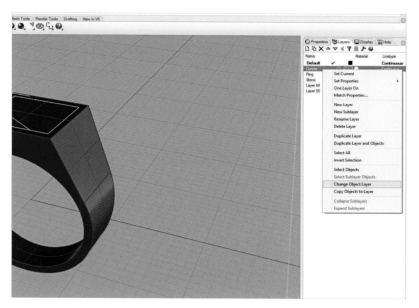

23 Put the rest of the curves in our Curves layer.

24 Copy the stone (Edit > Copy) and paste it in the Ring layer.

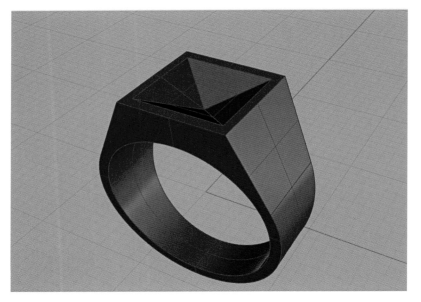

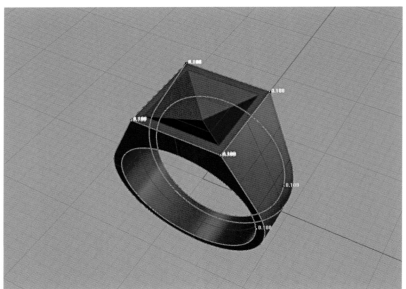

25 We will use the stone copy to subtract the shape from the main ring shape, thereby creating a depression for the actual stone, held in the Stone layer. Go to Solid > Difference, select the ring to subtract from and press [Enter], then the stone copy to subtract with and press [Enter] again.

26 To fillet the hard edges, starting with Solid > Fillet Edge > Fillet Edge, click on the Next radius option and set it to 0.1. Drag a selection around the whole ring, then deselect the edges on the stone depression by control-clicking. We don't need to drag any handles on this occasion, so skip the next prompt by hitting [Enter].

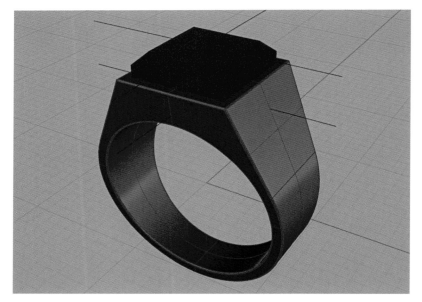

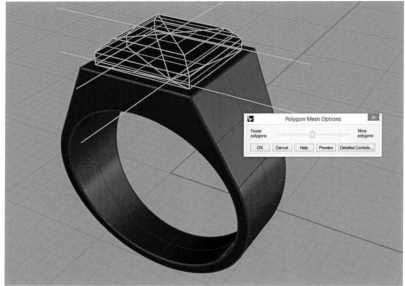

27 Turn both Ring and Stone layers on. Ne xt we will export the stone and the ring separately so that we can apply different material to them later.

28 Start by selecting the stone and going to File > Export Selected. Choose the .obj format, accept the default OBJ Export Options and the default number of polygons in the Polygon Mesh Options. Follow the same process to export the ring.

Octane interface

3

1 **2**^{A ¶} **4** **5** **6** **7** **8**

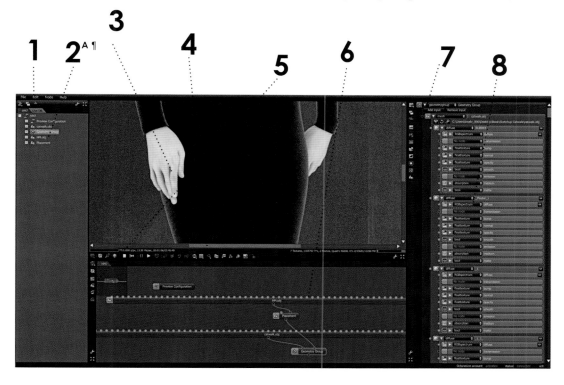

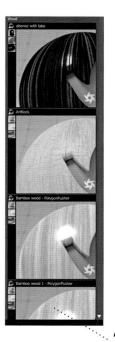

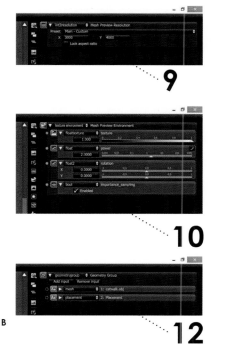

9

10

2^B

12

11

1 Main menu – This is where all of the commands can be found, separated into categories.

2 **A & B** Scene hierarchy panel and Live DB – A hierarchy of the scene so that objects can be selected by name, and a database of material presets.

3 Render view – This is where interactive rendering (IPR) is displayed.

4 Render view toolbar – These are commands that apply in the render view.

5 Node panel toolbar – This toolbar contains tools that apply to the node panel.

6 Node panel – This is a view of all of the elements in a scene in the form of visual nodes.

7 Panel icons bar - These icons open up different panels.

8 Current mesh panel – This panel includes options for the appearance of meshes (3D objects).

9 Resolution panel – This panel includes resolution options.

10 Environment panel – This panel includes HDRI (image-based) lighting options.

11 Kernel panel - This panel includes various rendering options.

12 Geometry panel - This panel includes options for objects in a scene.

1 Right-click in the Node Inspector and select Add Node > geometry > mesh. Browse for the 'ring.obj' file. If you cannot see the ring in the render view, click on the Camera View Presets button, select Front View, and zoom out (mouse-wheel) until you can see the ring.

2 Follow the same process to load the 'diamond.obj' file.

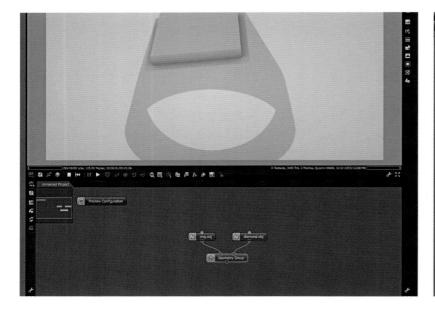

3 To make a group node to combine them, go to Add Node > geometry > geometrygroup. Click on the output dots of the ring and stone models and drag onto the Geometry Group node's input dots. Click on the Geometry Group node to display in render view.

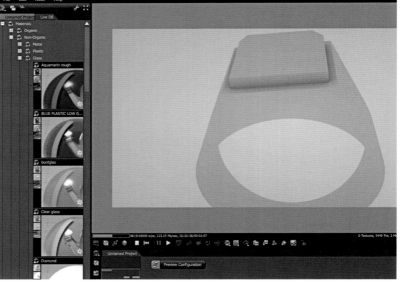

4 In the Outliner, click on the Live DB tab, and browse through the Non-Organic > Glass materials to find the Diamond material.

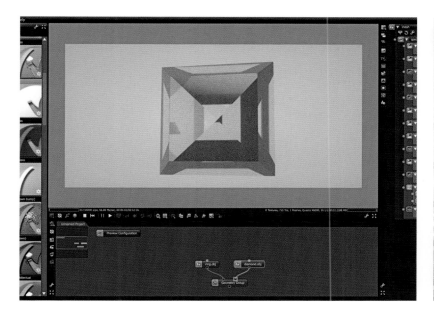

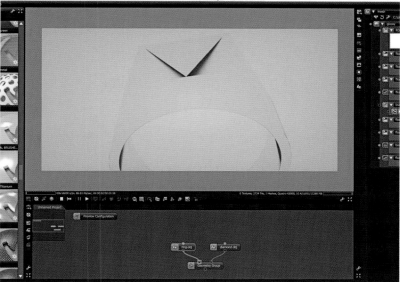

5 Select the diamond.obj node, right-click on the diamond material, select Copy from the pop-up menu, right-click on the stone model's material sphere in the Node Inspector and select Paste from the pop-up menu. The model will update to the diamond material in the render view.

6 Similarly, browse for the platinum material in the metal presets of the Live DB, copy and paste it onto the ring model's material sphere.

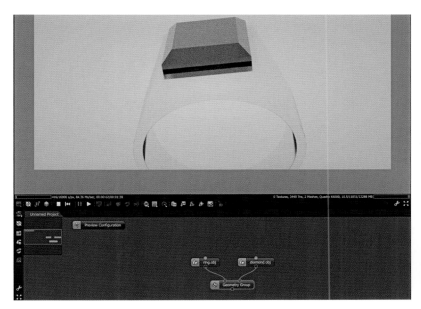

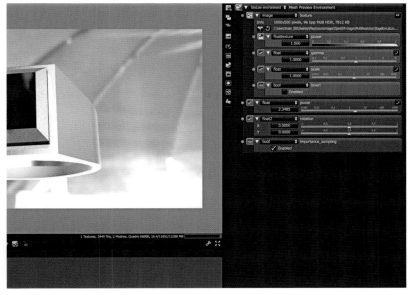

7 Click on the Geometry Group node to display both models simultaneously.

8 Click on the Environment icon on the right of the render view, click in the texture drop-down menu, set it to 'image', and load an .exr file. The render view will update so the lighting for the scene now comes from the .exr image.

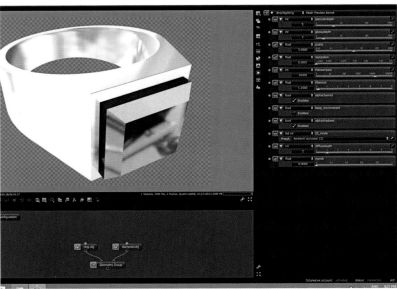

9 Click on the Resolution icon on the right of the render view and from the presets menu select a digital camera resolution (the higher the better, but also the slower to render).

10 Cick on the Kernel icon on the right of the render view and check the 'Enabled' box in the 'alphachannel' section. This will remove the background.

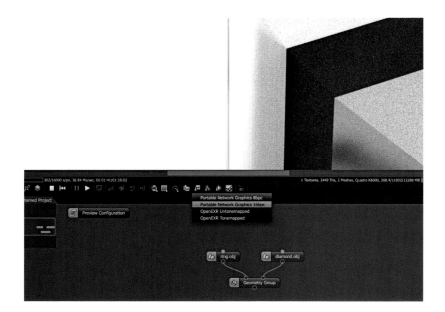

11 Click on the 'Save Render to Image File' button at the bottom of the render view and select the 'Portable Network Graphics 16bpc' from the drop-down menu.

Creating a bag with Rhino

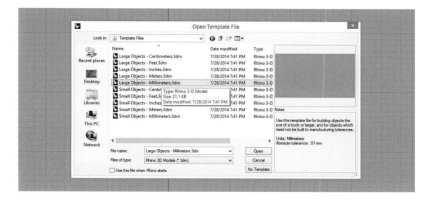

1 Go to File > New and select the Large Objects – Millimeters template.

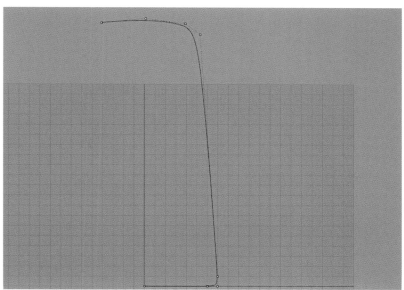

2 In the right view, select Curve > Free-Form > Control Points, click once at the origin and place points to create a shape similar to the illustration to create the profile of the bag. Place more points together for tighter curves, but avoid placing too many points. Also make sure that the last point intersects the vertical (green) axis.

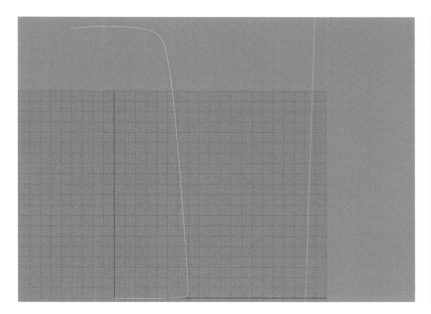

3 We'll now use a straight line to trim the shape (Curve > Line > Single Line). Draw the line on the vertical axis, intersecting the whole shape.

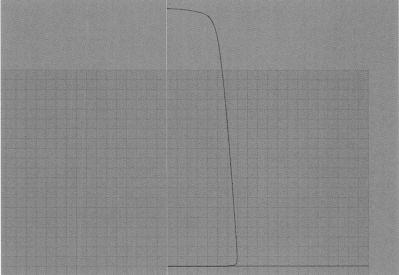

4 Use Edit > Trim, select the straight line as the cutting object, and any excess to the left as the object to trim.

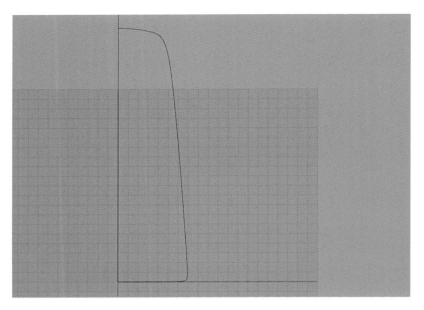

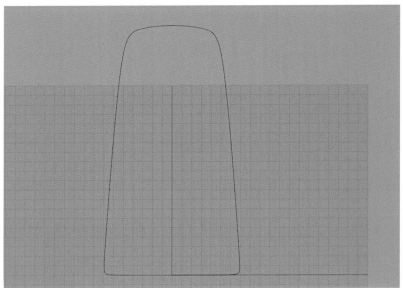

5 Next, go to Transform > Mirror and select the right half of the profile as the object to mirror. The start and end of the mirror plane will be anywhere on the vertical axis. We can now delete the vertical line.

6 Edit > Join the two pieces together.

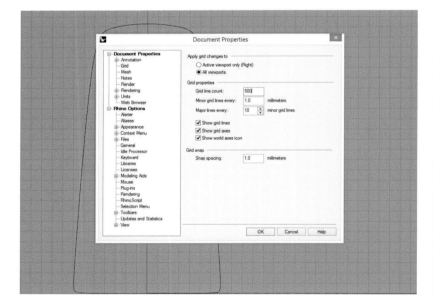

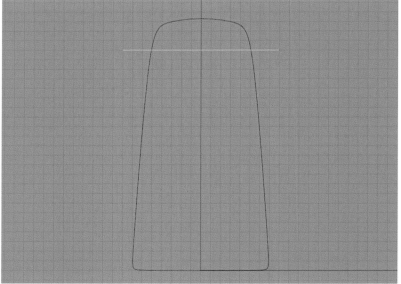

7 The bag profile now extends beyond the grid, and so extending the grid will make things easier. Go to File > Properties and in the Grid section of the Document Properties, change the Grid line count to 500.

8 Go to Curve > Line > Single line again and create a horizontal line this time, near the top of the bag profile.

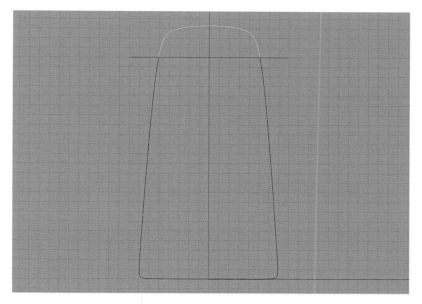

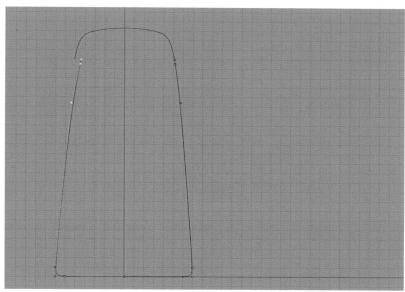

9 Use it as a cutting object to Edit > Split the top from the rest of the profile.

10 Turn the Control Points on for the bottom half of the split profile (Edit > Control Points > Control Points On). Drag-select the top few points of the left side of the bottom half of the profile and drag them slightly to the right. Then Edit > Control Points > Control Points Off.

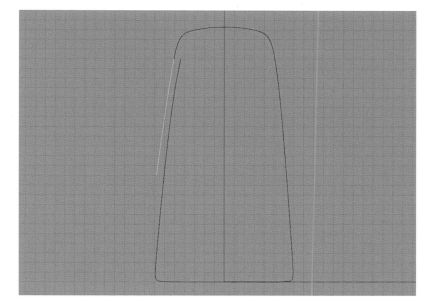

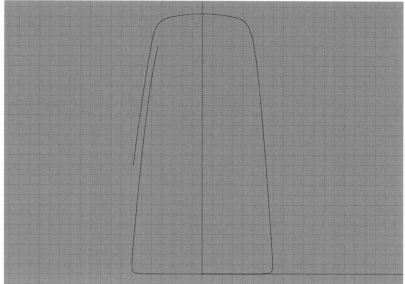

11 Using the Curve > Free-Form > Control Points tool, turn on End snap at the bottom of the screen (click on Onsnap if you can't see it) and start a new curve on the left endpoint of the top part. Extend the curve a little lower than the middle of the bag profile.

12 Edit > Join the new curve to the old curve.

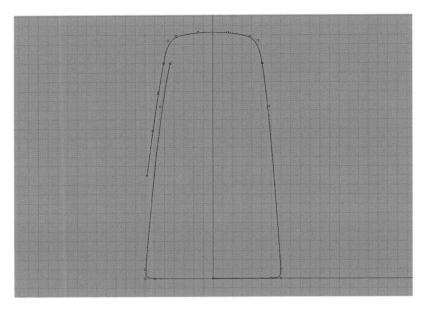

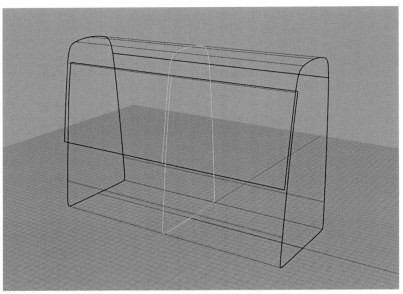

13 Turn the control points on for the combined curve that we now have, and with the selection arrow, select and delete any excessive points (eliminate clusters). Edit > Undo if deleting a point changes the shape of the curve drastically.

14 In the perspective view, select Surface > Extrude Curve > Straight, and extrude on both sides (BothSides = Yes) by 100mm.

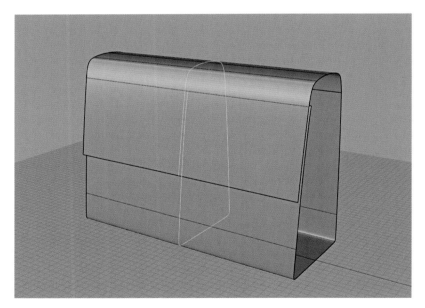

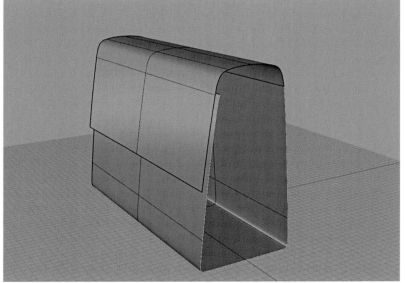

15 Right-click on the Perspective view title and select the Shaded display mode.

16 We'll now extract an edge from the edge of our surface. Go to Curve > Curve From Objects > Duplicate Edge, select the edge of the bottom part of the bag, and hit [Enter].

90 Creating accessories and jewellery

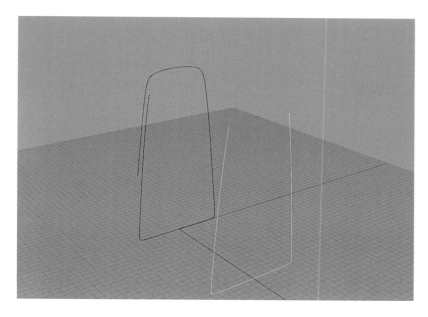

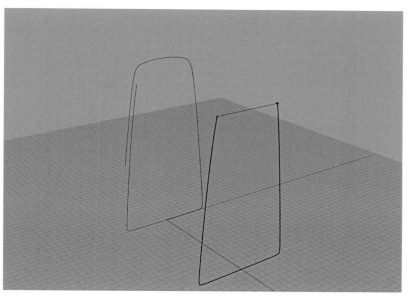

17 Select the surface and Edit > Visibility > Hide, so that we can work on the new curve more easily.

18 Make a straight line (Curve > Line > Single Line) from one to the other end of the edge we just extracted – make sure the End snap is on.

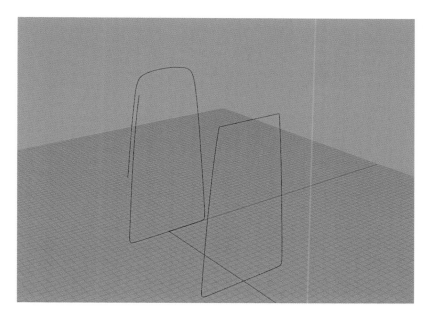

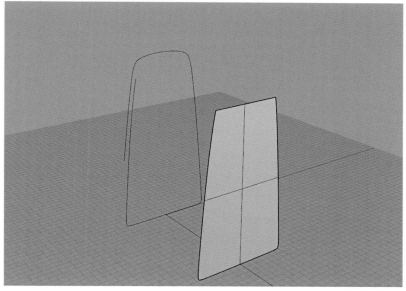

19 Join the new line with the curve.

20 We'll now make a surface out of this closed curve with Surface > Planar Curves. Select the closed curve and press [Enter].

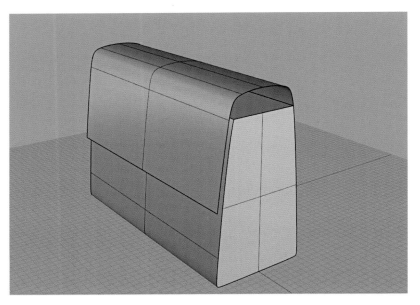

21 Edit > Visibility > Show to make the previously hidden surface visible again.

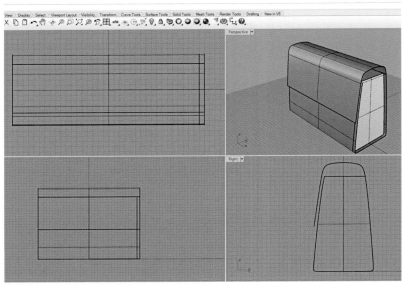

22 In the four-view layout, Transform > Move the side surface 10mm in – use the Grid Snap and drag, or type in the value.

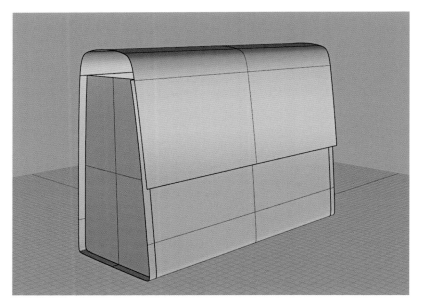

23 Transform > Mirror the new side surface over to the other side, using the vertical axis as the mirror plane.

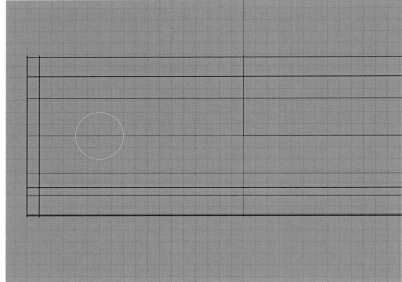

24 We'll now make some holes in our bag surface. In the top view, go to Curve > Circle > Centre, Radius, position the centre of the circle in the middle of the bag vertically, and about 60mm in from the left end. Give it a radius of 20mm.

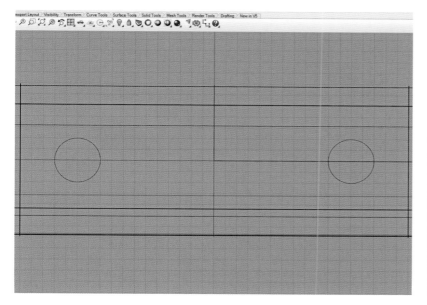

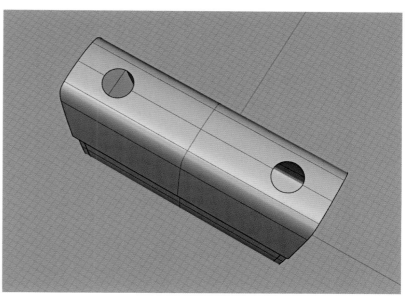

25 Mirror the circle over to the other side, using the vertical axis as the mirror plane.

26 Use the Edit > Trim command in the top view, with the circles as cutting objects, to trim the surfaces of the bag inside the circles.

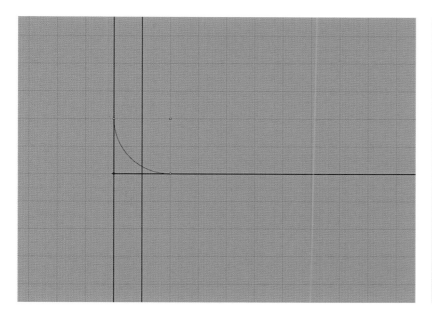

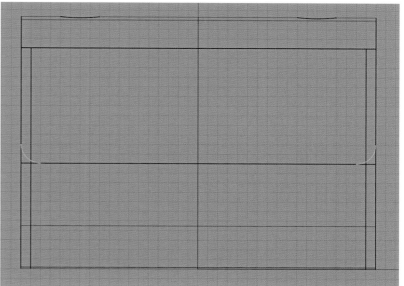

27 We'll now curve the corners of the flap of the bag. In the front view, go to Curve > Arc > Start, End, Direction, place the start of the arc 2mm higher than the corner of the flap, and the end of the arc 20mm to the right of the corner of the flap.

28 Drag from the end of the arc to the corner of the flap to define the direction of the arc and then copy-mirror the arc over to the other side.

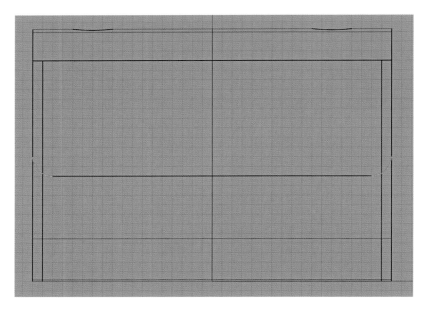

29 Trim the corners of the flap, using the arcs as cutting objects.

30 In the front view, make a circle around the middle of the flap with Curve > Circle > Centre, Radius. Give it a radius of 10mm.

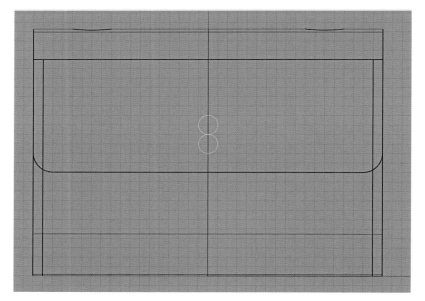

31 Transform > Copy the circle 2cm lower, so that the second circle touches the original.

32 Now draw two lines connecting the sides of the circles (Curve > Line > Single Line).

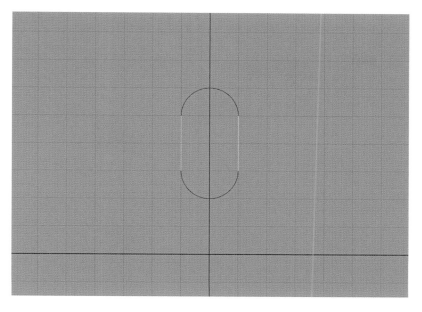

33 Trim the inside of the circles.

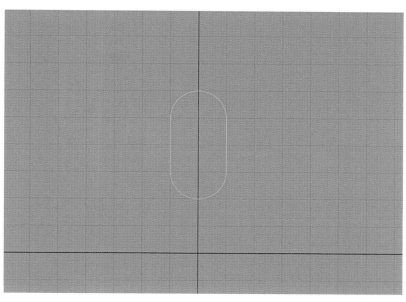

34 Join the circle and line segments together.

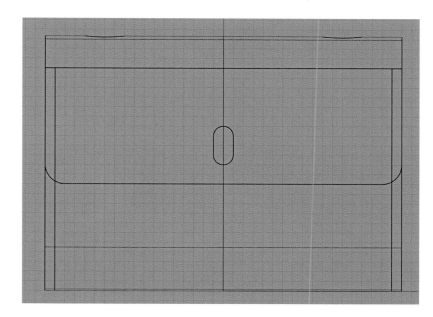

35 Use the Trim command and the curve we just created as a cutting object to trim the surface of the flap enclosed in it.

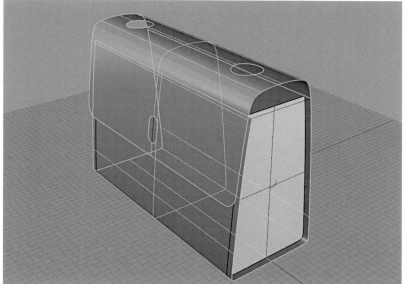

36 Join the flap surface with the rest of the bag.

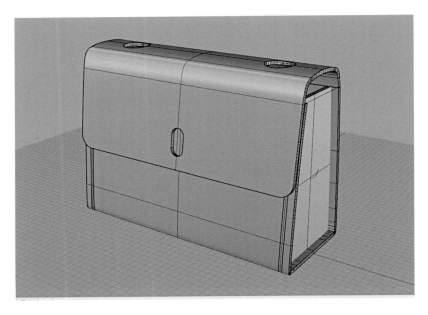

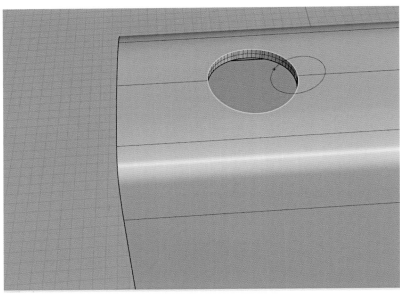

37 Go to Surface > Offset Surface and select the bag surfaces. Make sure that all arrows look inwards. If not, click on the Flip All option in the command line. Type in 5mm for thickness and press [Enter].

38 Go to Solid > Pipe, select the upper edge of the left hole in the top of the bag and press [Enter]. Type in 10mm and press [Enter] again.

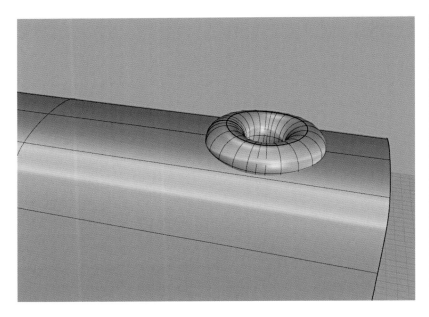

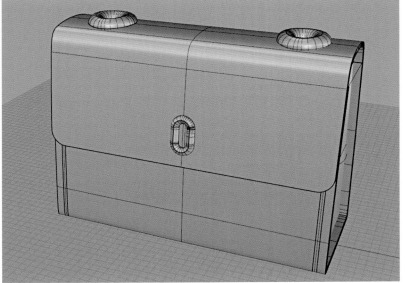

39 Repeat for the other hole.

40 And the same for the hole in the front of the bag, this time with a radius of 5mm.

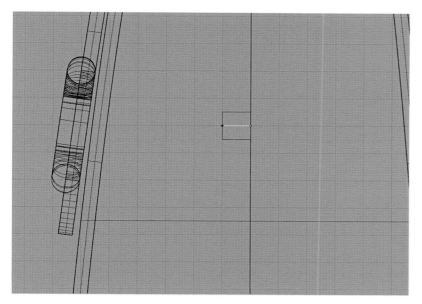

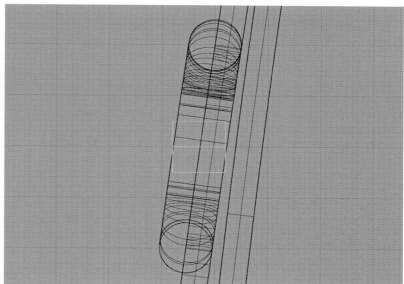

41 Use Solid > Cylinder to make a cylinder in the middle of the flap hole – place the base in the middle with Grid Snap and set the radius to 5mm. Move to the right view, and you will notice that the cylinder starts on the vertical axis. We'll move it in a minute, but for now, hold [Shift] and click 10mm to the left.

42 Transform > Move the cylinder from its base (use Grid Snap) to the centre of the flap hole.

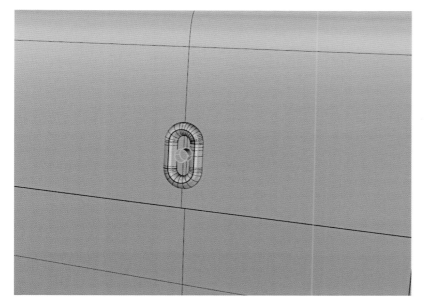

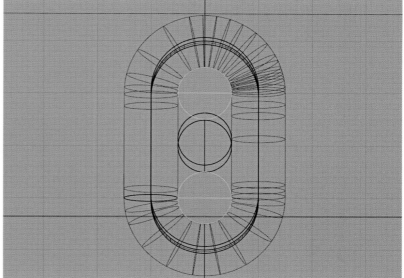

43 Transform > Rotate the cylinder with the centre of rotation at the base of the cylinder, the first reference point at the other end of the cylinder (hold [Shift] while doing this), and the second reference point so the cylinder sits within the hole's pipe profile.

44 To create the latch, start by making a sphere (Solid > Sphere > Centre, Radius). Position the centre of the sphere in the centre of the top arc of the latch hole, and give it a radius of 5mm. Repeat to make another sphere at the centre of the bottom arc.

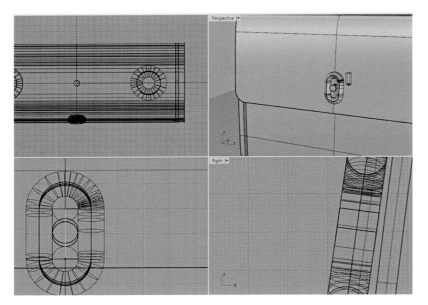

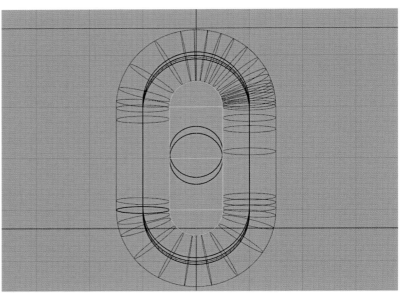

45 Go to Solid > Cylinder, position the base of the cylinder at the centre of the top sphere, make the radius 5mm, and position the end of the cylinder at the centre of the bottom sphere.

46 Let's combine the cylinder with the spheres. Go to Solid > Union, select both spheres and cylinder and press [Enter].

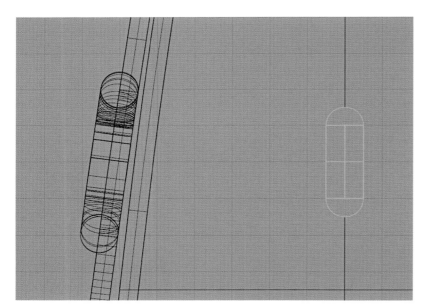

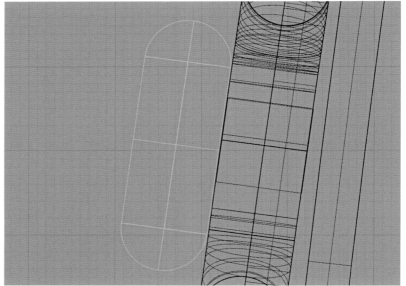

47 All new shapes are created by default on the plane of the view used, so we must move the new solid to the desired position. Transform > Move, select the solid, click at its centre with Grid Snap on, then click in front of the latch to place it there.

48 Transform > Rotate in the right view, click in the middle of the right side of the capsule solid to define the centre of rotation, hold [Shift] and click to the left of the solid to define the first reference point, then slightly higher to align with the latch hole pipe.

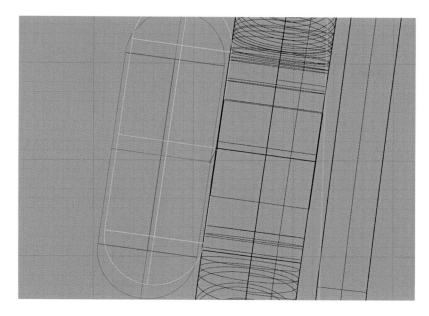

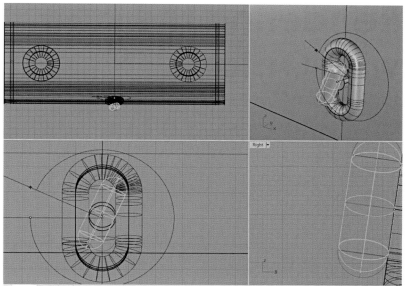

49 You may need to move the solid slightly to perfectly align it with the centre of the latch. Go to Transform > Move, select the solid, and move it so that it is positioned right against the latch, exactly in the middle of it.

50 Now we will rotate the solid to close the latch. In the perspective view, go to Transform > Rotate 3-D, place the start of the rotation axis at the centre of the base of the horizontal cylinder (use the Centre Snap option in the Osnap – Object Snap – options bar at the bottom of the screen), and the end of the rotation axis at the centre of the top of the horizontal cylinder. In the front view, define the first reference point anywhere around the capsule solid, then rotate until the solid is horizontal and click to define the second reference point.

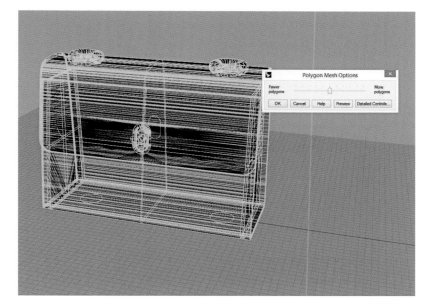

51 File > Save As to save the Rhino file, then File > Export Selected, select only the main bag shape, and save the file in .obj format with the default options. Repeat for the metallic details (save them all in one file).

Rendering the bag with Octane

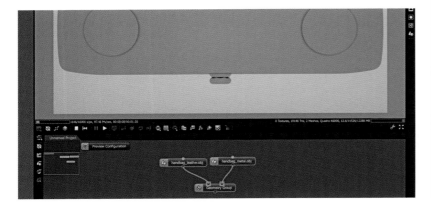

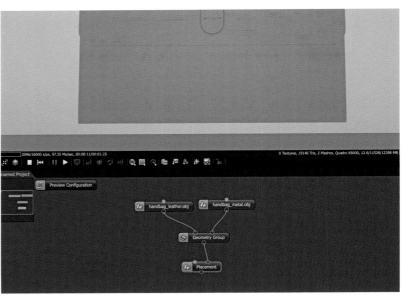

1 Now for the bag, create a new document (File > New), load the leather and metal parts separately, and combine them with a Geometry Group. Select the front view from the view drop-down menu and zoom out until you see the entire bag.

2 TThe bag must be rotated, so right-click in the nodes view and introduce a Geometry > Placement node. Feed the output of the Geometry Group into the input of the Placement node, and change the X value of the Rotation section to -90.

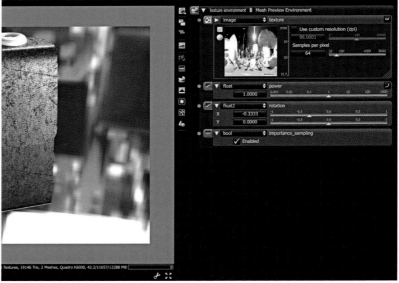

3 Apply a leather material to the bag and a metal material to the hard parts.

4 In the Environment section, set the texture to 'image' and load an .exr file.

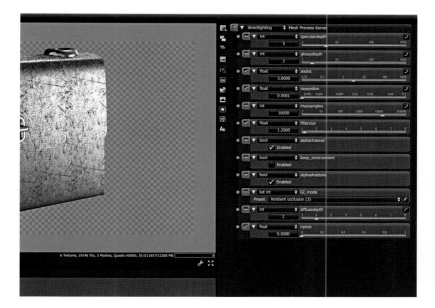

5 In the Kernel section, turn the alpha channel on.

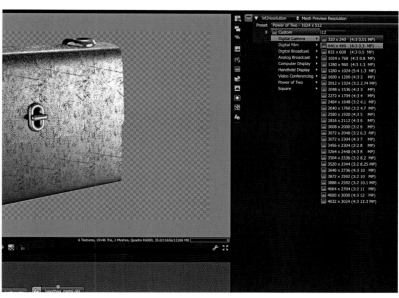

6 In the Resolution section, select a digital camera preset.

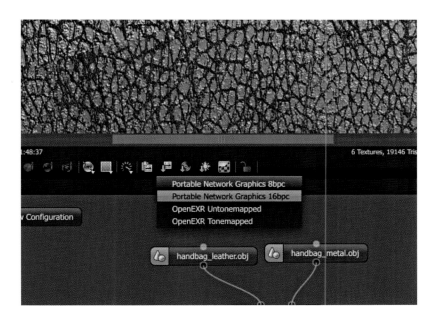

7 Save the image as a 16bit PNG, as before.

Final
project

Constructing a Gabrielle Miller Dress

In the final project, we will go through the whole process of producing a 3D fashion visualization. The design is by fashion and textile designer Gabrielle Miller. We will import the patterns into Marvelous Designer, adjust them, sew them together, place them on an animated mannequin, and simulate the draping. We will also make a hat to go with the dress. The design will finally be exported from Marvelous Designer and imported into Maya, where it can be textured and rendered, using the IrayForMaya renderer, which is based on NVIDIA's very successful Iray shading system. The tutorials can be downloaded from the website listed in Resources (page 173).

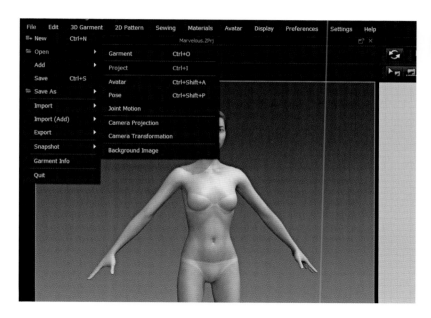

1 Go to File > Open > Project, and open the CLO3D document that we previously saved in CLO.

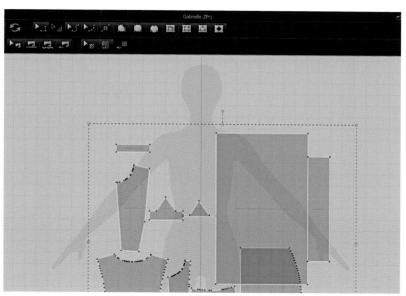

2 With the Transform Pattern tool, select all of the pieces and scale them down to the size of the mannequin.

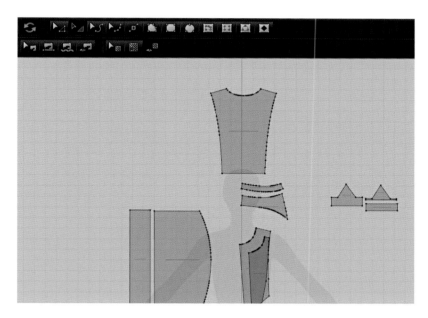

3 Using the same tool, select and move the pieces around to lay them out as in the illustration.

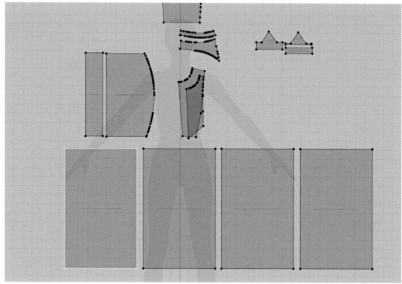

4 Right-click on the rectangular skirt piece and select Copy from the drop-down menu. Right-click next to it and select Paste. Position the copy next to the original and repeat two more times to have four pieces altogether.

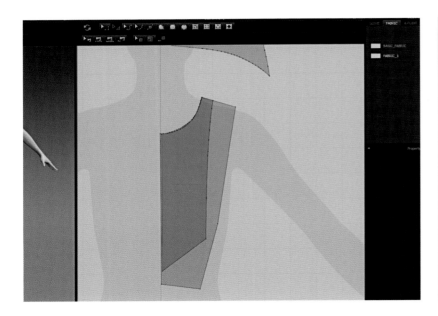

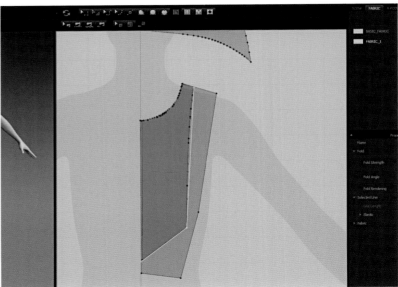

5 Move the small decorative bodice piece inside the larger base one and align them.

6 With the Internal Polygon tool, trace the inside of the small shape on the larger base shape. With the Edit Curvature tool, curve the straight lines to make them the same as the curves of the small shape.

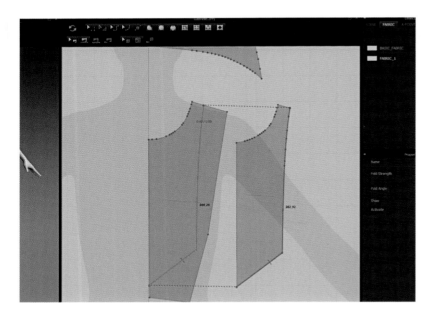

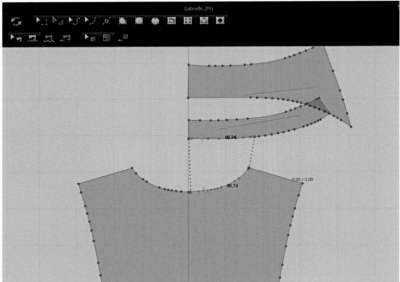

7 Move the small piece back to the side of the larger piece, and with the Free Sewing tool, sew together the inside seams from top to bottom, then do the same with the outside seams.

8 Move the collar pieces above the back bodice piece and sew half of the half collar base to the right of the bodice collar edge. Then sew the top of the collar to the top of the collar base.

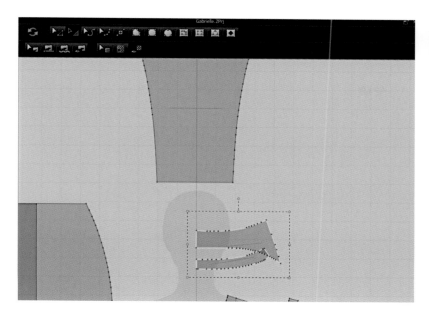

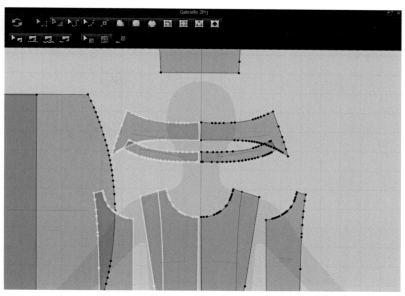

9 Select the collar pieces and move them above the front bodice pieces.

10 Select the front bodice and collar pieces and mirror-copy them. The seams are copied with the pieces so there is no need to sew anything on the copies.

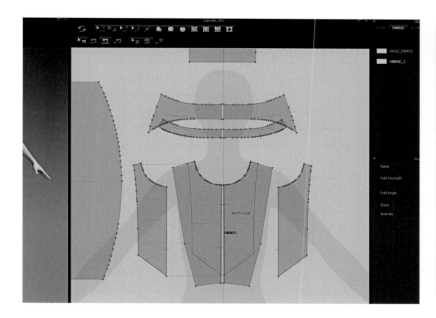

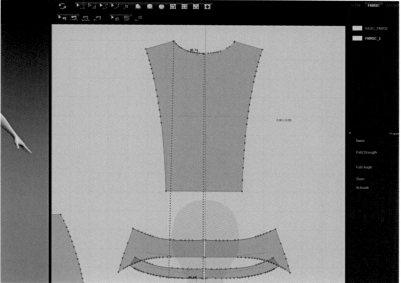

11 Now create the front seams for the collar and bodice pieces.

12 The inside half of the bottom edge of the collar base piece has to be sewn to the left collar edge of the back of the bodice.

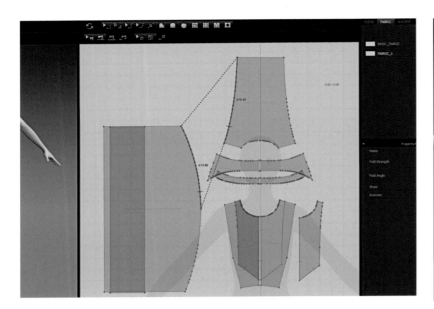

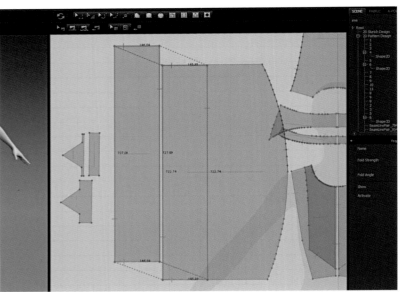

13 Sew the inside bottom half of the sleeve to the outside edge of the left half of the bodice. Rotate the back of the bodice by 180 degrees and sew its left edge to the inside top half of the sleeve.

14 Create an internal rectangle at the end of the sleeve of the same size as the separate piece for the inside of the end of the sleeve. Then sew all sides of one to the other.

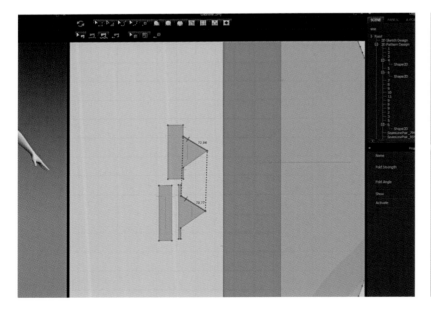

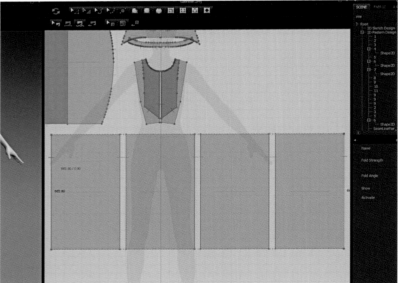

15 Sew the two decorative top pieces of the cuff to the base of the cuff.

16 Sew the sides of the skirt pieces together.

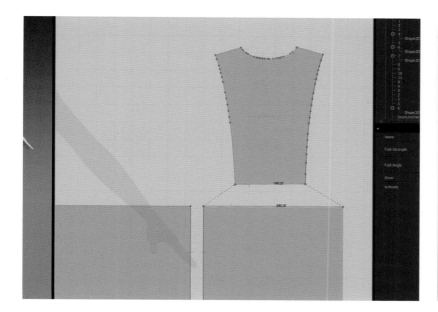

17 Use the Add Point tool to place a point in the middle of the top edge of the front skirt piece. Sew the bottom edge of the front left bodice piece to the left segment and the right to the right.

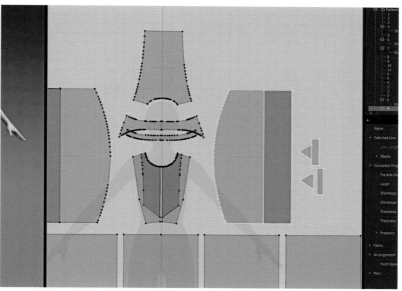

18 Put the back bodice piece upright above the back skirt piece and sew the two together. Then rotate the bodice and put it back above the collar.

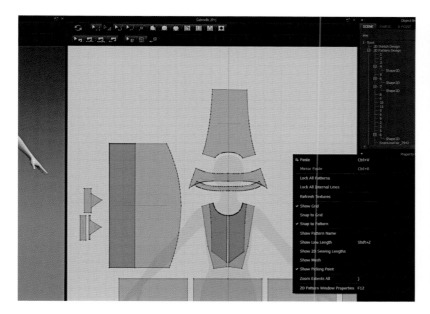

19 Mirror-copy the sleeve pieces and place the copies on the right side of the bodice.

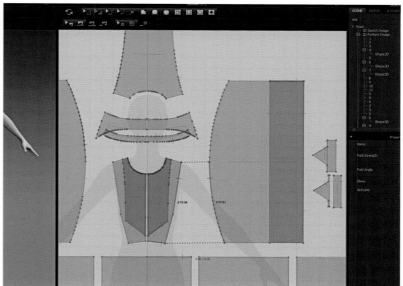

20 Sew the base of the mirrored sleeve to the front and back of the bodice.

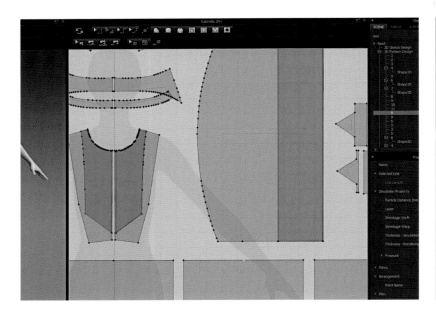

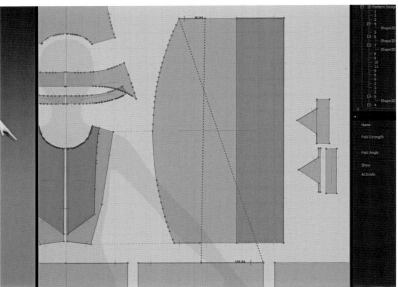

21 Place a point on the bottom edge of the right sleeve, around 80mm from the left corner. Then place a point in the middle of the top edge of the corresponding skirt piece. Sew the left segment of the latter to the left segment of the former.

22 Place a point on the top edge of the right sleeve, around 80mm from the left corner. Then sew its left segment to the right segment of the top of the skirt piece below, making sure that the seam is flipped.

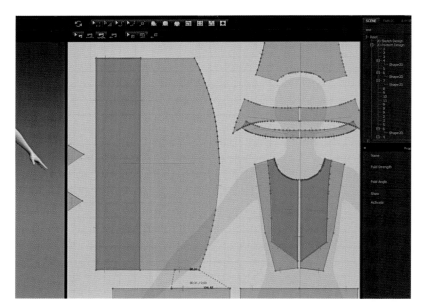

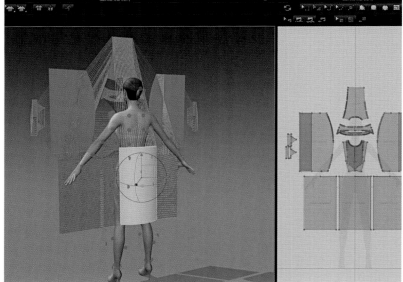

23 Do the same for the left sleeve and the corresponding skirt piece.

24 Press the Sync button to place the patterns in 3D view. Turn arrangement points on (second button from top, top left corner of 3D view), click on the back skirt piece, orbit to see the back of the mannequin, click on a back arrangement point to place.

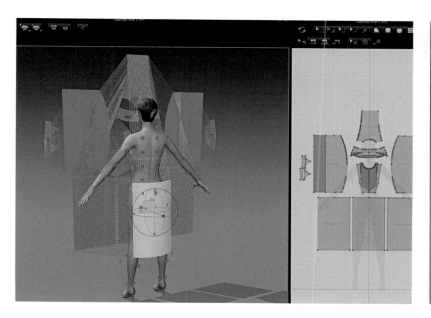

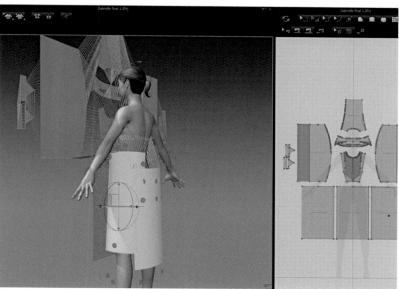

25 Go to Preferences > Gizmo and select the World Coordinate gizmo, which moves and rotates based on the world axes – this is a matter of preference but I find it much easier than the other options. Use the gizmo to move the skirt piece a little lower.

26 Place the side skirt piece on the side of the mannequin using a placement point and then the world gizmo.

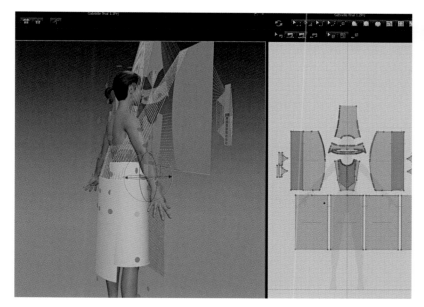

27 Do the same for the other side skirt piece ...

28 ... for the front bodice pieces (select base and decorative pieces one side at a time) ...

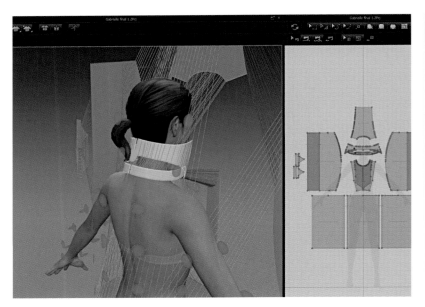

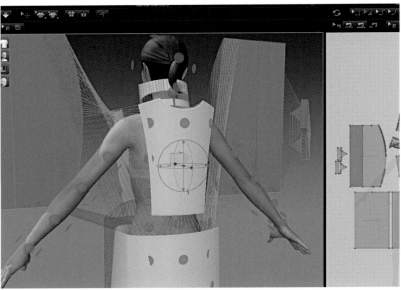

29 ... for the collar pieces (select all of them and place them using the neck back arrangement point) ...

30 ... for the back bodice piece (you will also have to rotate this) ...

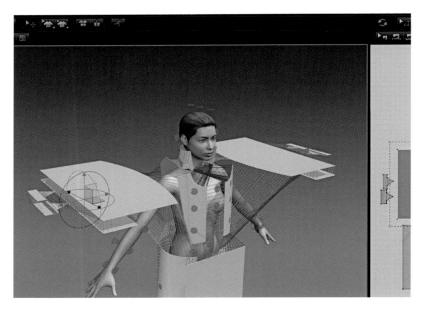

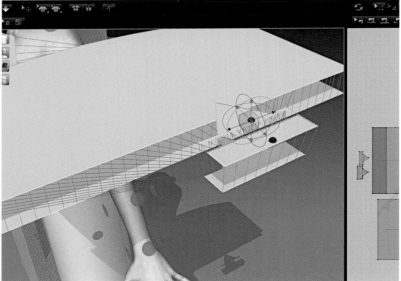

31 ... and for the sleeves (select all of the pieces together for each side).

32 Separate the outside from the inside pieces.

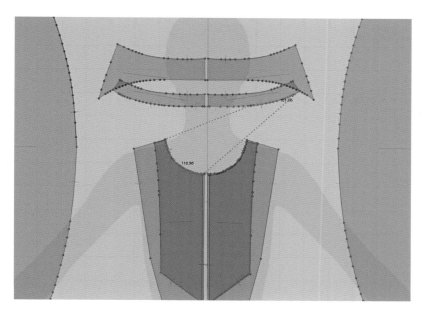

33 Sew the outside segments of the bottom edge of the collar base to the opposite collar segment of the front bodice.

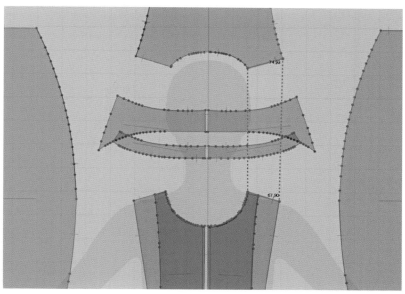

34 Sew the front and back bodice pieces together at the shoulders.

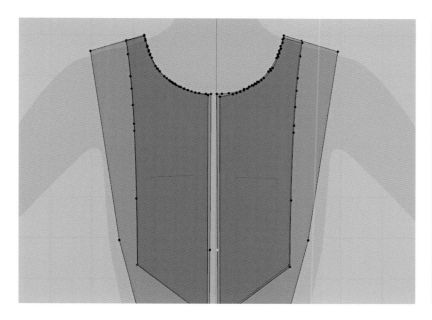

35 We'll now have to open up the chest part of the collar. Place a point on each side of the chest opening, about two thirds down the opening, and sew together the lower segment.

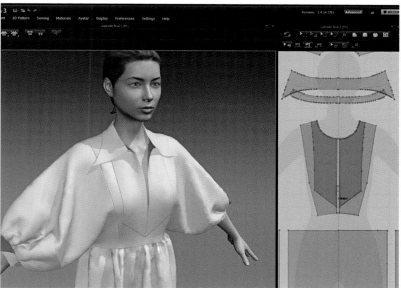

36 Sync and play the simulation, and the chest parts will update.

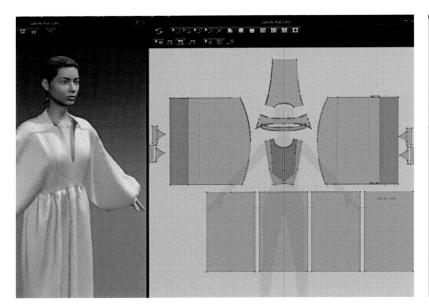

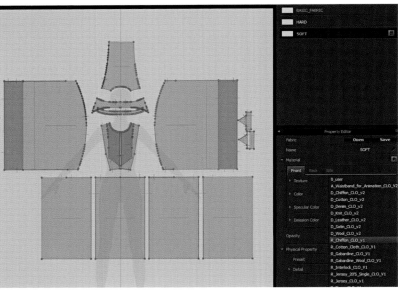

37 With the component tool, select the wrist points of the main (large) sleeve pieces, and drag them outwards to elongate the sleeves, as they are currently too short. Play the simulation again to update the design.

38 Make two new fabrics in the Fabric tab of the Object Browser (click the Add button) and call them 'hard' and 'soft'. In the Property Editor, scroll down to the material presets, and give the hard fabric a leather material and the soft fabric a chiffon material.

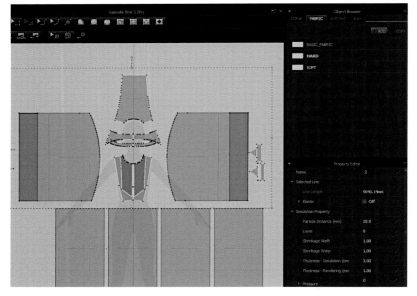

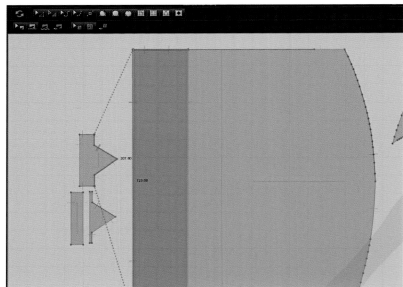

39 Drag-select all of the pieces and drag and drop the soft fabric to the selection. Select all of the 'hard' parts (shown in the illustration) and drag and drop the hard fabric to them.

40 Use the Free Sewing tool to sew the inside of the wrist base to the end of the sleeve.

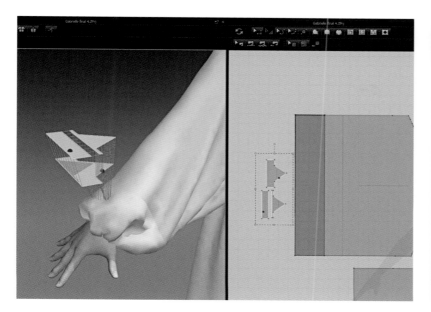

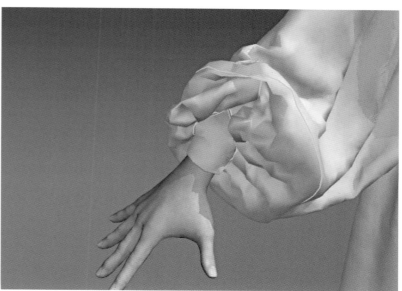

41 Pause the simulation, select the wrist pieces in the 2D view, move them apart form the rest of the dress in the 3D view using the world gizmo, right-click on them and select Reset 3D Arrangement (Selected).

42 Start the simulation again. The wrist pieces will wrap around the end of the sleeve.

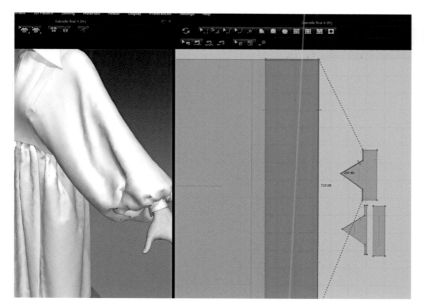

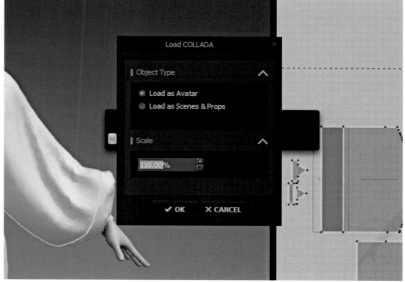

43 Do the same for the other wrist/sleeve.

44 Let us now import our animated avatar. Go to File > Import > Collada, browse for and open the avatar Collada file, and select Load as Avatar. The default size of 100% should be fine, but if not, reload and adjust the size.

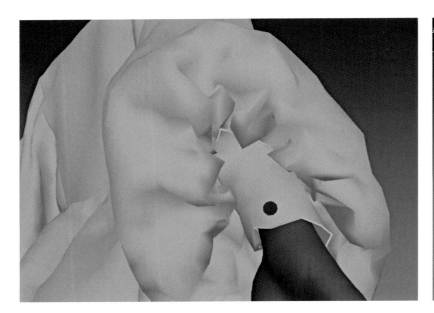

45 Place the draped pieces around the new mannequin with the world gizmo (imported avatars do not have arrangement points), and adjust the 2D patterns if needed to fit the new body. Re-simulate and pull in the 3D view if needed.

46 A very small seam can be added on the back of the collar to keep it in place.

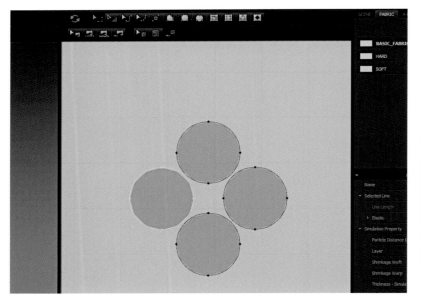

47 Use the Circle tool and copy/paste three times to make four small circles side by side diagonally.

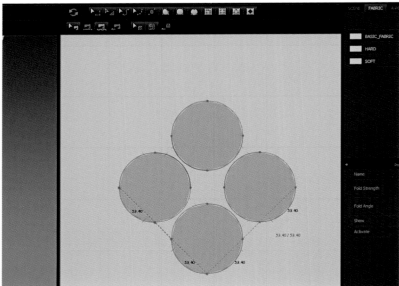

48 Sew the inside and outside segments of the circles together.

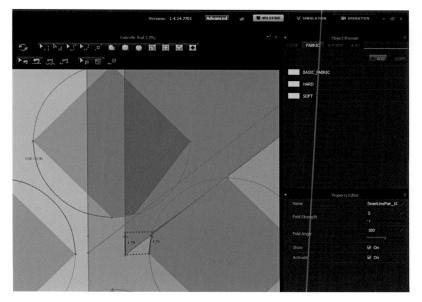

49 Scale the circles down and stitch one of the inside segments to the base of the chest decoration with a very short seam. Select the circles in the 2D view and in the Property Editor, set the Pressure attribute either to 100 or to -100, depending on whether the circles face the right or the wrong way out (white or grey).

50 Now select the circles in the 2D view and place them on top of one another. This will make duplicating and placing them easier.

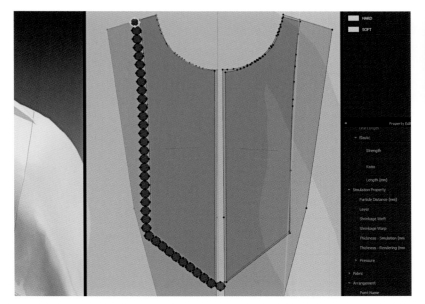

51 Copy and paste until you have a whole series of decorative spheres along the outside of the decorative piece.

52 Select and mirror-paste the spheres (all but the very bottom one) in the 2D view, then position them in the 3D view with the world gizmo.

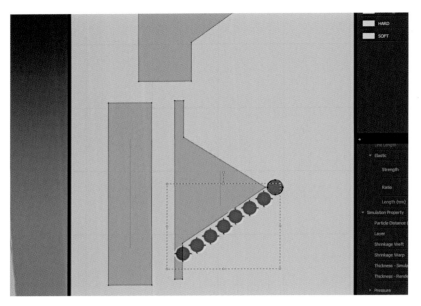

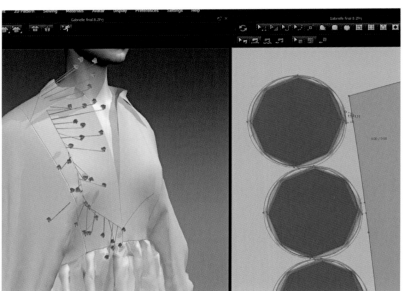

53 In the same way, create a series of spheres along the wrist decoration.

54 Stitch all of the balls to the edges of the chest and cuffs decorative pieces with tiny seams.

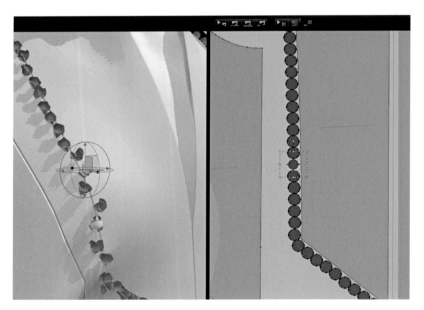

55 Select all of the balls that face the right side out (white) and turn the Pressure attribute in the Property Editor up to 100. Select all balls that face the wrong way out (grey) and turn the Pressure down to -100. This will inflate them.

56 Go to the Animation side of the programme – click on the Animation button in the top right corner of the interface – make sure the simulation quality is set to Complete, and hit Record to play and record the animated simulation.

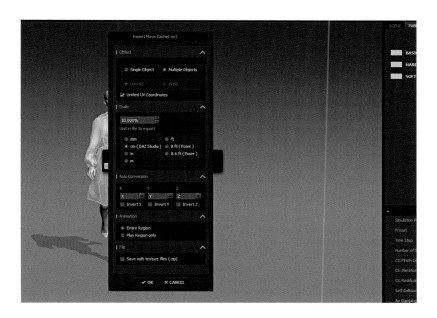

57 Once the simulation is completed, go to File > Export > Maya Cache to export the animation for use in Maya. In the options box, select Multiple Objects, Unified UV Coordinates, cm (DAZ Studio), and hit OK. An .obj file will also automatically be saved with the Maya cache in this case.

58 To save a static .obj to shade and render in another program (such as Maya or Octane), place the playhead where you want it in the animation to get a good pose, go to File > Export > OBJ, and in the options box select: Select All, Multiple Objects, Thin, Unified UV Coordinates, and cm.

Making a hat

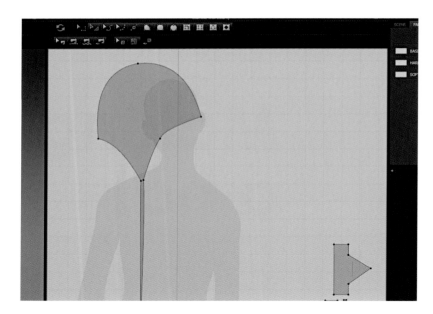

1 With the Polygon tool, create a very basic shape that represents the start of half of the hat. Use the Edit Curvature tool to bend the lines. You may also want to add more points and/or to manipulate points with the Edit Pattern tool.

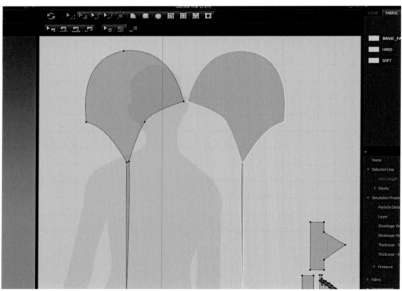

2 Copy and mirror-paste the half opposite the original.

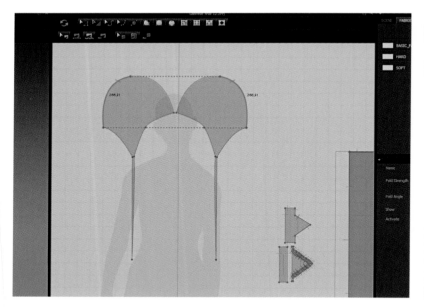

3 Sew together the top round segments.

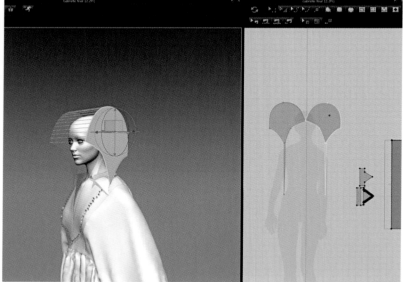

4 Sync the 3D view, place the halves on each side of the head, and play the simulation. Resize appropriately in the 2D view and drag in the 3D view to make the hat suit the mannequin's head.

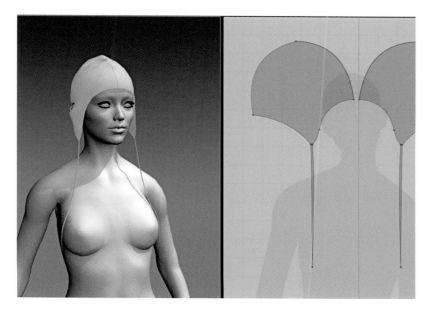

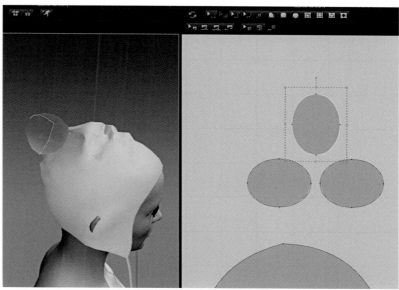

5 Refine the patterns by pulling the points and the curves. Make a new fabric, call it 'Wool', give it a wool preset, and apply it to the hat patterns.

6 To create the pom-pom for the top of the hat, create a small circle, copy it twice, sew together the inside and outside segments, elongate them as in the illustration, and stitch the inside of one of the circles to the top of the hat using a very short seam. Make a new fabric, call it 'pom-poms' and apply to the pom-pom.

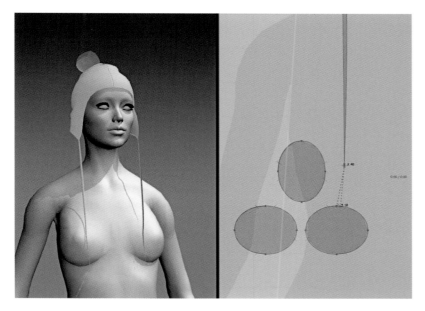

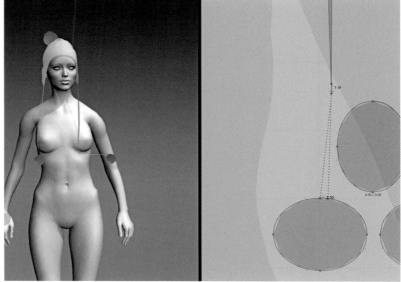

7 After that, select the pieces and change their Pressure attribute to 100 or -100 depending on whether they face the right (white) or wrong (grey) side out. Make a copy of the three circles (the whole pom-pom) and sew them to the end of the flap.

8 Do the same for the other flap.

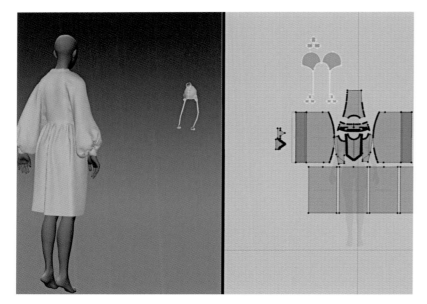

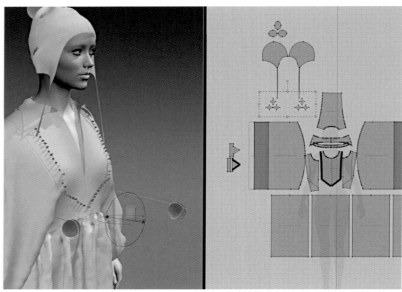

9 Save the hat (Save As > Garment) and open the dress document (File > Open > Project). Then File > Add > Garment and open the hat document to add it to the existing scene.

10 Pick the Word Coordinate gizmo (under Preferences > Gizmo) and use it to move the hat in place. Also, drag the pom-poms in front of the dress if they are intersecting the mannequin.

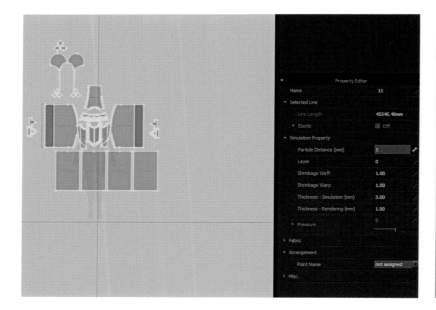

11 Select all of the patterns in the 2D view, and in the Property Editor, change the Particle attribute (under Simulation Property) to 5. This will give us a much more accurate simulation.

12 Record the simulation and save the Maya cache or the OBJ model as before.

Creating a scene and rendering with Maya and Iray

Maya is one of the most prominent software packages for visual effects (VFX) for film and electronic entertainment. It is used for modelling, animation, character creation, particle effects, and many other purposes. In this tutorial, we will use Maya to create a scene including the mannequin that we previously exported from Daz (complete with shoes and hair), the garment that we exported from Marvelous Designer, and the ring that we exported from Rhino3D. We will then apply materials and textures to all of the objects. We will use IrayForMaya, a plugin renderer for Maya created by German-based company [0x1], which is based on NVIDIA's Iray framework for shading and rendering. The tutorials can be downloaded from the website listed in Resources (page 173).

Maya interface

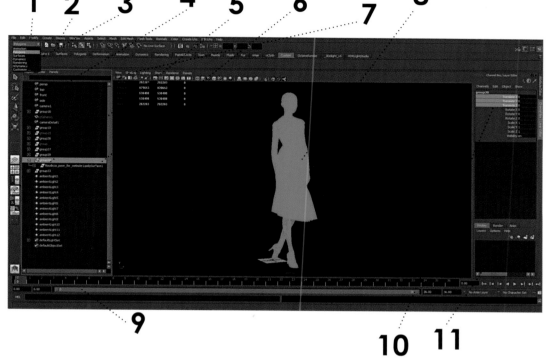

1 Main Menu – This is where all of the commands can be found.

2 Status Bar – Contains shortcuts for menu items and tools for object selection and snapping.

3 Menu Sets – These are sets of task related tools, such as Modeling and Animation.

4 Tool Box – Contains Maya's most common tools, such as Select, Move, Rotate, and Scale.

5 Quick Layout Buttons – These switch between Maya's predefined panel layouts

6 Outliner – This offers a hierarchy of the scene so that objects can be selected by name.

7 Viewport Menu – These are menus for operations in individual views.

8 Viewport – This is where the 3D scenes are navigated and manipulated.

9 Time Slider and Range Slider – These define the playback range and current time of an animation.

10 Channel Box - The Channel Box allows the editing of values for selected objects.

11 Layers – This panel shows Display Layers for scene management and Render Layers for setting up render passes for compositing.

12 Hypershade and Hypergraph – These display networks of nodes, such as shading materials.

13 Attribute Editor – Allows the editing of attributes of objects.

14 Render View – This is where interactive rendering (IPR) and final rendering are displayed.

15 UV Texture Editor – This is where the UV coordinates of models are laid out for texturing.

12

13

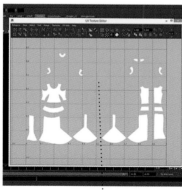

14

15

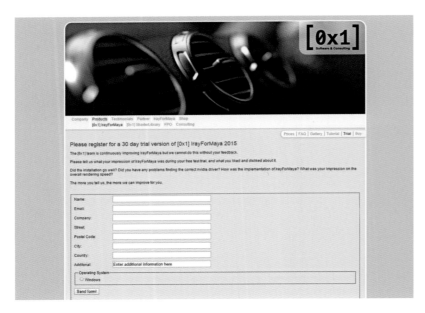

1 To download a 30-day trial of IrayForMaya, go to the following address on the [0x1] website: http://www.0x1-software.com/en/produkte/0x1-irayformaya/testen.html. Double-click on the file and follow the onscreen instructions to install it.

2 To load the plugin in Maya after it has been installed, go to Window > Settings/Preferences > Plugin Manager and in the Plugin Manager window, scroll down to see the IrayForMaya plugin. Check both boxes next to it and close the window.

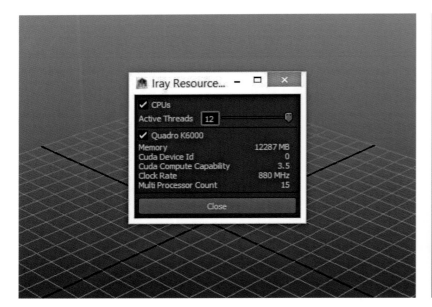

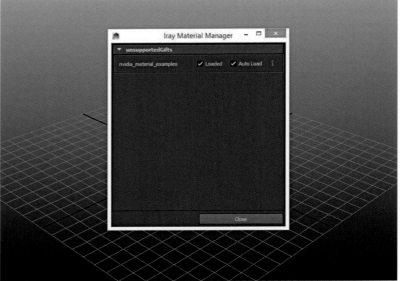

3 You also need to go to Window > Rendering Editors > Iray > Resource Manager and make sure that both CPUs and NVIDIA cards are selected to maximize rendering performance.

4 Finally, in the Material Manager in the same Iray menu, make sure that the two boxes for the material examples are checked.

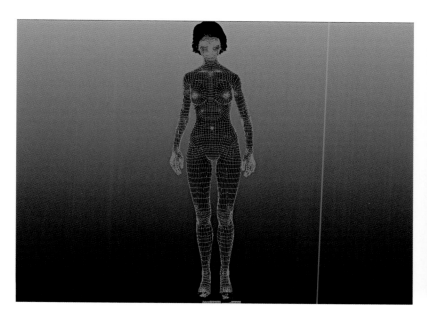

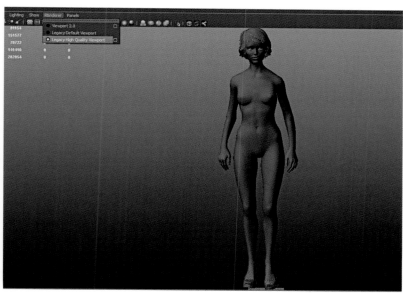

5 Let's go to File > Import to import our mannequin. FBX and Collada formats will all work here as exported from DAZ Studio, but in this example I have chosen to use the Alembic format (.abc).

6 On some setups the mannequin geometry may display wrong. If this happens, in the viewport menu, under Renderer, select the Legacy High Quality Viewport option.

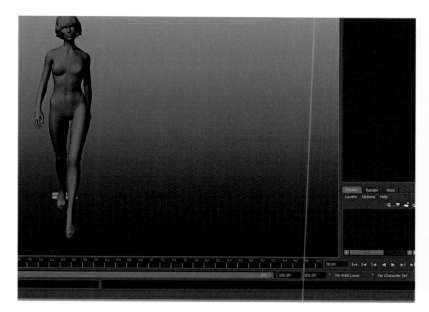

7 Change the number of total frames in the timeline to the total number of frames in the mannequin animation. I have 100 frames in this example. Drag the playhead to check that the animation works.

8 Go to File > Import again, and this time load the outfit OBJ that we previously exported from Marvelous Designer. This static .obj does not include any animation.

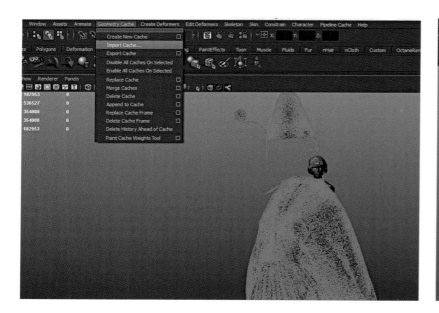

9 To load the cloth simulation animation from Marvelous Designer, select the outfit with the selection tool and also select the Animation menu from the menus drop-down menu in the top left corner of the screen. Then go to Geometry Cache > Import Cache and select the XML file previously created for the outfit in Marvelous.

10 In some cases, the outfit may be at a different scale to the mannequin. Select the outfit and adjust its size in the Channel Box. I set the Size X, Y and Z to 0.909.

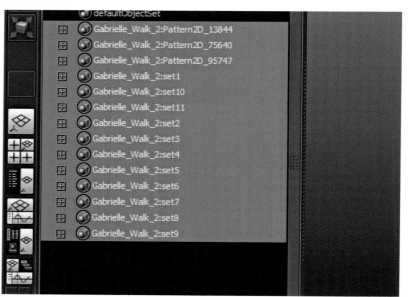

11 Select the hair and press [Delete] to delete it. We will not need it for this project.

12 Click on the third from the top interface layout to turn on the Outliner, select all of the lighting and shading nodes and delete them, as we will not need them.

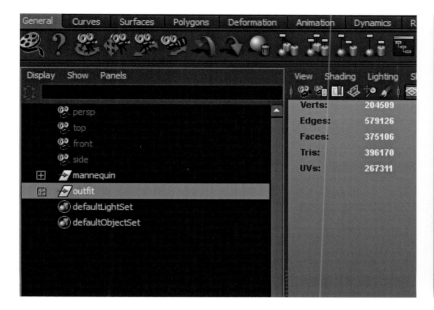

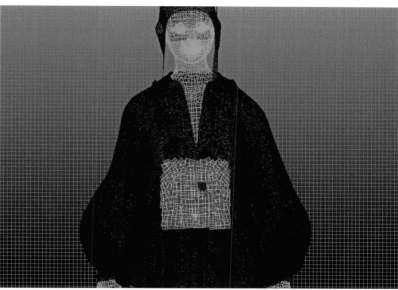

13 Still in the Outliner, click on the two groups and rename them 'mannequin' and 'outfit' so that we can recognize them.

14 This step is only necessary if parts of the mannequin intersect the dress. In the front view, right-click on the mannequin and select Face from the pop-up menu. Press [4] on the keyboard to go into wireframe mode, drag-select the polygons that are covered by the dress and hit [Delete] to delete them.

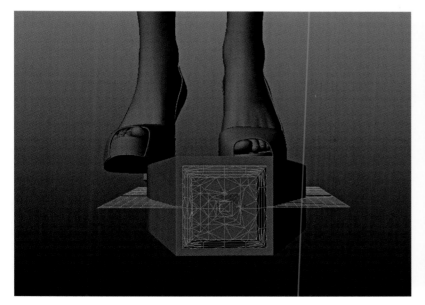

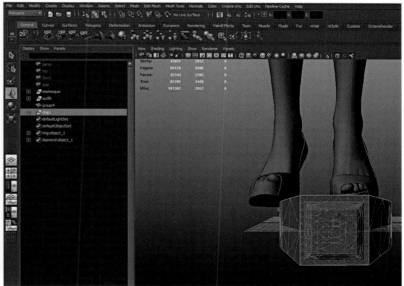

15 It is time to import the ring (File > Import) and select the .obj format and the ring file, then repeat for the stone file. Rename them 'ring_base' and 'diamond' in the Outliner.

16 Shift-select and Edit > Group the two, then rename the group 'ring'.

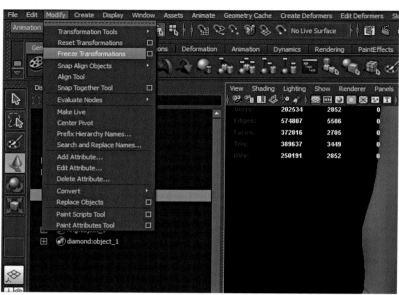

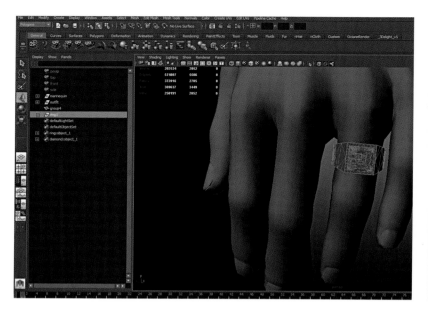

17 Use the Move, Rotate and Scale tools to place the ring around a finger.

18 With the ring group selected, go to Modify > Freeze Transformations to reset Translate and Rotate to 0, and . Scale to 1.

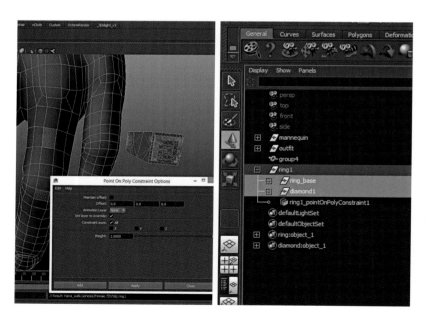

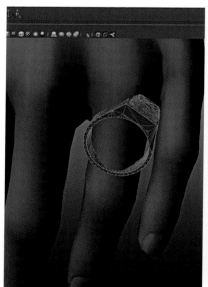

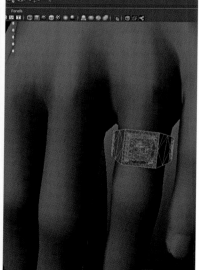

19 Right-click on the hand, go into Face mode, select a face on the finger, SHIFT-select the ring, and go to Constrain > Point on Poly. In the Outliner, shift-select the 'ring_base' and 'diamond' and Edit > Group them into a new 'ring_rotation' group.

20 Select the new group and go to Modify > Centre Pivot; by default, new groups have their centre at the origin/centre of the scene). Move and rotate to fit the ring around the finger; drag the playhead in the animation timeline so the ring follows the finger.

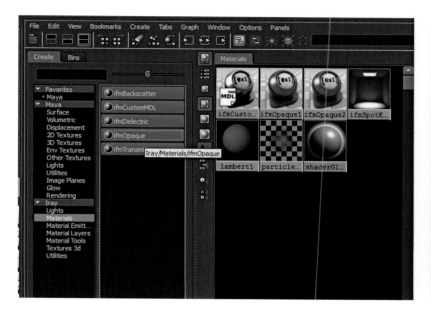

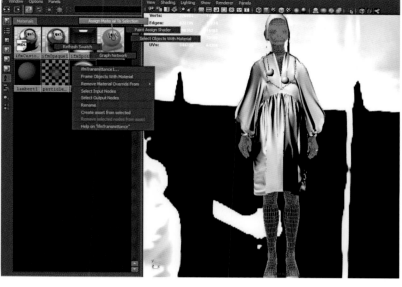

21 In the Hypershade (fifth layout preset), expand the Iray section, click on 'Materials', then select the ifmOpaque option to create a new material node. Select all geometry (outfit and mannequin), hold-right-click on the new material and choose 'Assign Material to Selection' from the pop-up menu.

22 In the Iray section of Hypershade, click on Lights, then select ifmImageBasedLighting. Change over to the Outliner, double-click the newly created light node, and in the Attribute Editor on the right, click on the folder and load an EXR image to use as the light source.

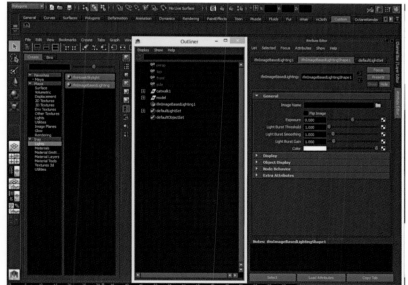

23 Click on Open Render View icon, and inside select the Iray option from the renderer drop-down menu, and hit the IPR render icon to render the perspective view. Check that the greys are not too dark nor light, and adjust the Exposure of the light.

24 Create an ifmTransmittance material, select the mannequin, hold-right-click on the material and select 'Apply Material To Selection'. Double-click the material and change its diffuse colour in the Attribute Editor to H:24.270, S:0.146, V:1.

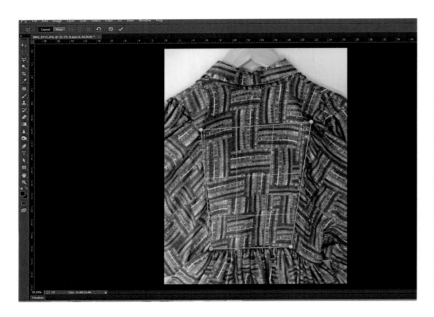

25 In Photoshop, load the photograph of dress back and go to Edit > Perspective Warp. Position the corners of the box as above (an almost rectangular section), click on the Warp button in the options bar, and drag the box corners near the edges to straighten the fabric pattern as much as possible; click tick to confirm.

26 Vertical and horizontal guides can be placed by clicking on the rulers around the document (press [Ctrl]+[r] on PCs or [Cmd]+[r] on Macs if the rulers are off) and dragging into the document. The guides can be moved, locked, or cleared from within the view menu.

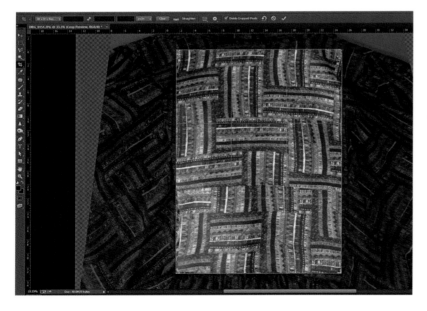

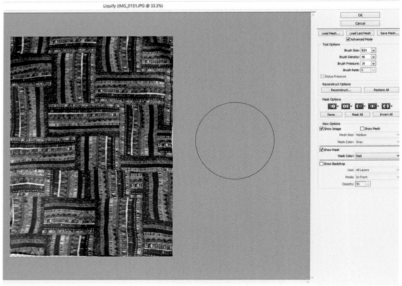

27 Use the Crop tool all the way to the edges of the document and confirm ([Enter] or the tick icon) to get rid of the invisible out-of-bounds content.

28 Go to Filter > Liquify and in the Liquify interface, adjust the size and pressure of the brush, and push the uneven/wavy parts into place.

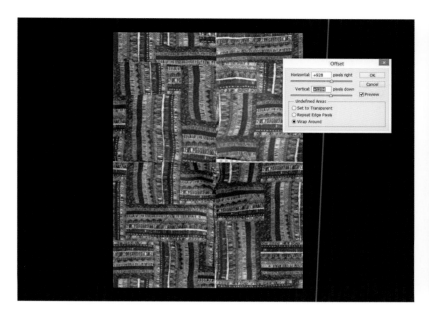

29 Now go to Filter > Other > Offset, and in the Offset dialogue, set the Horizontal and Vertical sliders so that the edges of the document are moved to its middle, and confirm.

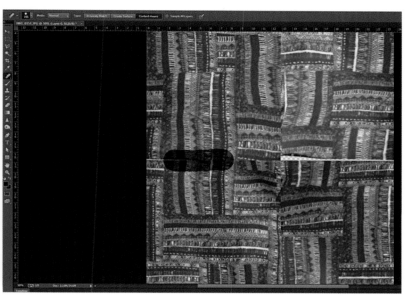

30 Now use the Spot Healing Brush tool with short strokes to cover up the seams.

31 Crop again if necessary.

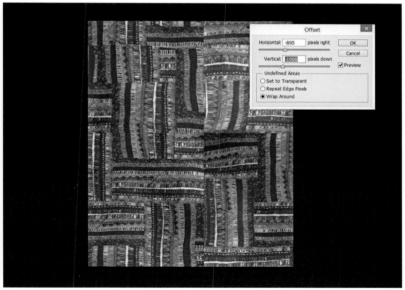

32 Offset again so that the edges are in the middle.

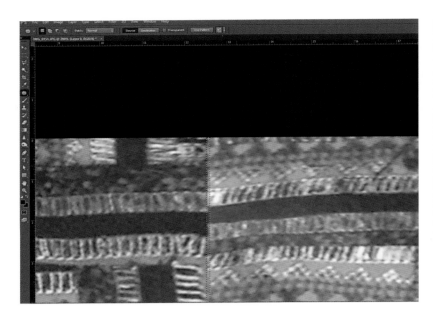

33 Use the Rectangular Marquee tool to select the area around a seam, then switch over to the Patch tool (in the same toolbar submenu as in the Spot Healing Brush tool), click inside the thin rectangular selection, drag to its side and release to use a sample. Repeat for all problematic areas.

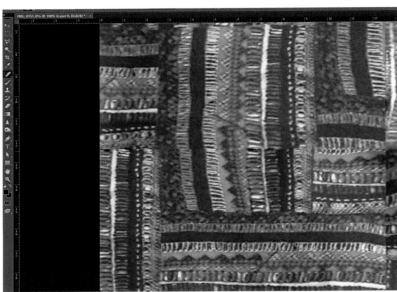

34 Use the Spot Healing Brush tool on the seams again if necessary.

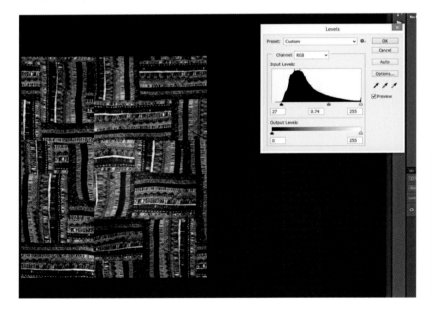

35 Go to Image > Adjustments > Levels, drag the shadow and highlight (black and white pointer) input levels to the start and end of the histogram, then the mid-tones (grey pointer) slightly to the right, to adjust the brightness and contrast of the fabric.

36 Run another round of the Liquify tool to iron out any wavy imperfections.

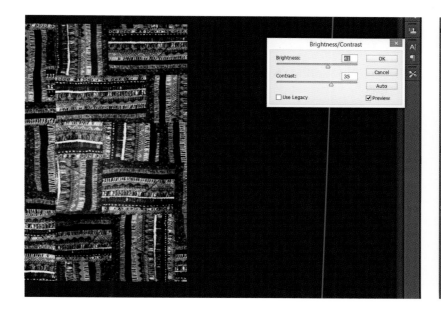

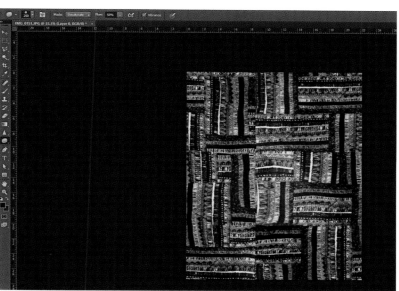

37 Use Image > Adjustments > Brightness/Contrast if necessary, to further enhance the fabric.

38 One area of the fabric looks more saturated than the rest, so we can use the Dodge tool to fix it. Select the tool and 'paint' on the oversaturated area until its saturation matches the rest of the fabric. File > Save As and save the fabric as a JPEG image.

39 Back in Maya, create a new Backscatter Iray material in the Hypershade, double-click it so that it comes up in the Attribute Editor, and rename it mainFabric.

40 Click on the chequered box next to the Color slider and select the File render node. The File node will now appear in the Attribute Editor. In File Attributes, click on the folder next to the Image Name field and load the fabric JPEG created in Photoshop.

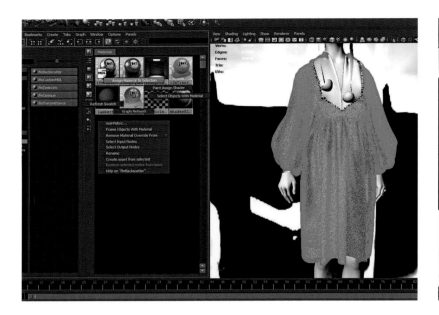

41 To apply the textured material selectively, select the outfit and use Mesh > Separate in the Polygons menu. Select pieces to be textured with our fabric material (use the Outliner if needed) and Edit > Group them; select group, hold-right-click on material in the Hypershade and select 'Apply Material To Selection'.

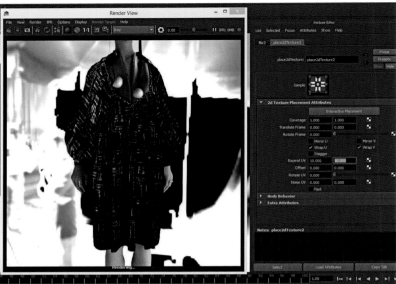

42 IPR render the view to see the new material applied. Its scale is wrong, so go into Attribute Editor with the material selected and in the Place2DTextureNode tab (to find this, click on the 'file' tab of the material, then click on the 'Go to output connection' icon), change the Repeat U and V attributes to 10.

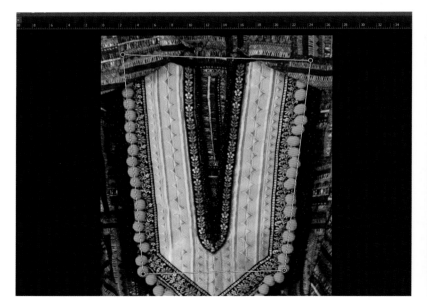

43 Load the image of the chest of the dress onto Photoshop, and use the Edit > Perspective Warp technique once more to fix it.

44 Select the decorative chest pieces and go to Window > UV Texture Editor.

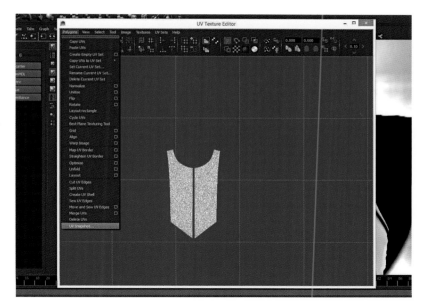

45 The UV Texture Editor will appear with the UVs of the selected pieces highlighted. Go to Polygons > UV Snapshot in the editor to save a snapshot for use in Photoshop. In the options box, define the save location, the size (I used 2048x2048), the format (I used BMP) and confirm.

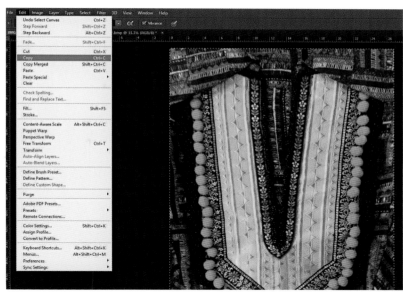

46 Go over to Photoshop and the chest image, Select > All and then Edit > Copy.

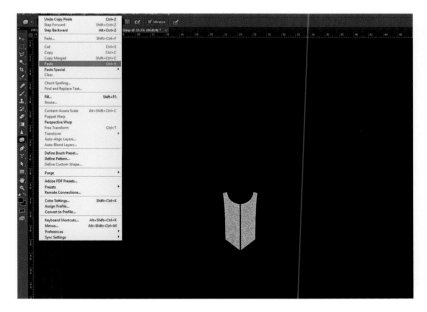

47 Load the snapshot (it will be in the directory you specified when you saved it) and go to Edit > Paste to paste the chest onto the snapshot.

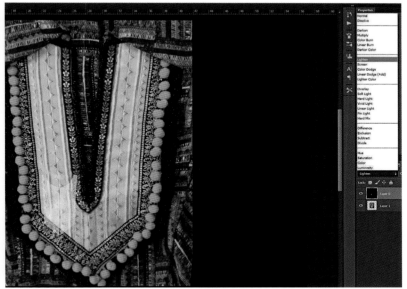

48 In Layers, double-click the background layer to unlock. Confirm the New Layer box, and click and drag the background layer (now called Layer 0) on top of Layer 1. Still in the same palette, click inside the layer modes menu and select Lighten.

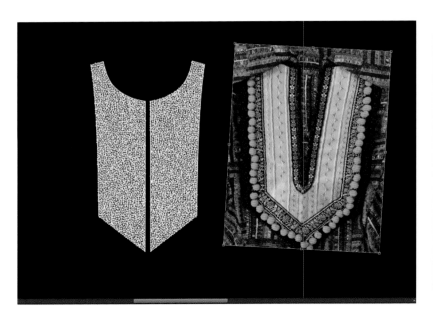
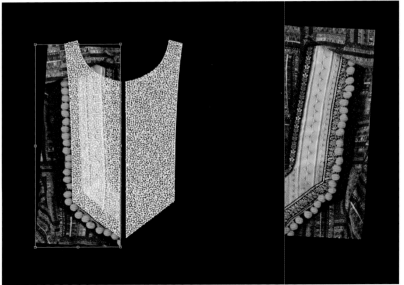

49 Select Layer 1, go to Edit > Free Transform, hold [Shift] and drag one of the corner handles of the layer inwards to make it the same size as the UV snapshot. Rotate it slightly if necessary using the same tool and use a guide to position it so that one side fits half of the UV outline. Press [Enter] to confirm.

50 Draw a rectangular marquee around the good half, cut and paste it. It will automatically be pasted on a new layer. Position it over the corresponding UV outline.

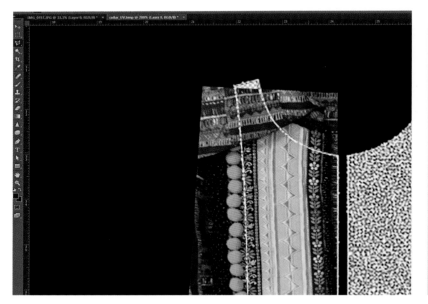
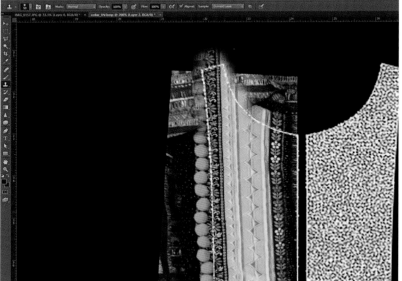

51 Select the UV layer and, with the Polygonal Lasso tool, draw a selection just inside its outline. Edit > Cut to get rid of the selection. This will make our work easier.

52 Using the Clone Stamp tool, alt-click to pick a sample area on the chest, then draw to duplicate that area to extend the chest to cover the whole UV outline area. The sample spot will always follow the tool pointer.

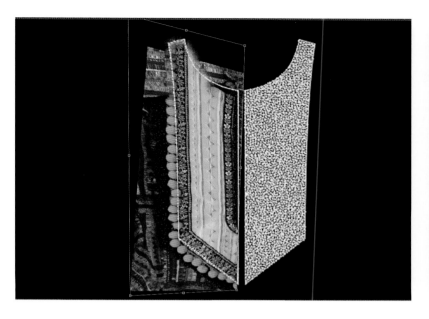

53 Using Edit > Perspective Warp, make sure that the inside fits the outline.

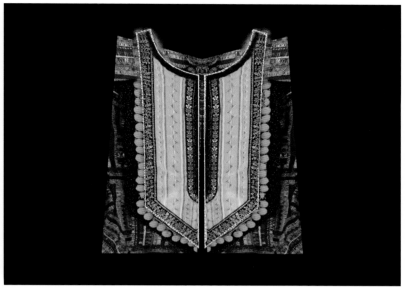

54 Edit > Copy, Edit > Paste Special > Paste in Place, and Edit Transform > Flip Horizontal and position the copy inside the corresponding UV outline.

55 Turn off Layer 0 that contains the UV outlines and save the document as a JPG and as a PSD in case further work is required later.

56 In Maya, select the chest pieces again and group them.

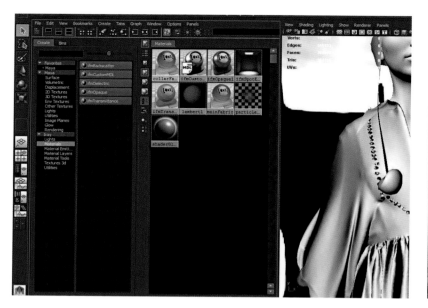

57 Create a new Backscatter Iray material, click on the checkered icon in the colour input and select File from the pop-up menu. In the file tab of the material in the Attribute Editor, click on the folder next the 'Image Name' and load the chest JPEG.

58 Select the chest group and apply the latest material to it. IPR render to see that the material is applied correctly.

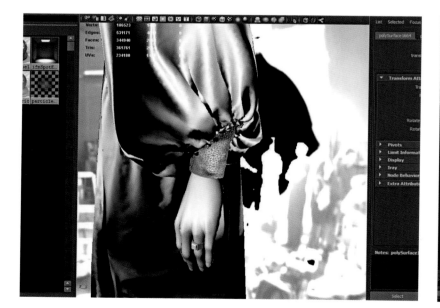

59 Now select the cuffs and go to Window > UV Texture Editor again.

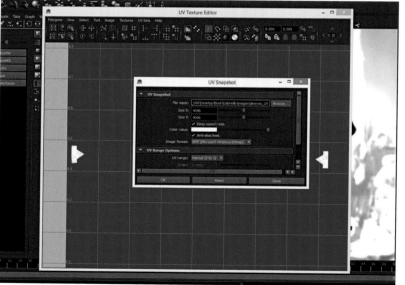

60 The pieces are highlighted in the editor. In the editor menu, go to Polygons > UV Snapshot once more. Select the file name and location, size (2048x2048) and format (BMP) and confirm.

61 In Photoshop, load the cuff image and draw a selection around it with the Polygonal Lasso tool.

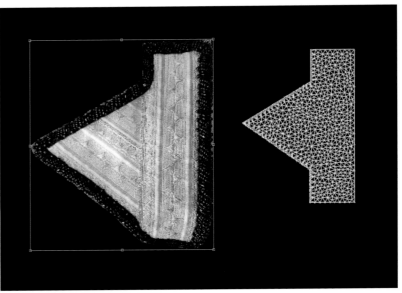

62 Load the new UV outline, and copy and paste the selection onto it. Adjust size, position and orientation.

63 Double-click on the background layer to unlock it and confirm the options box. Move Layer 0 (the background layer) to the top in the Layers palette and set its mode to Lighten.

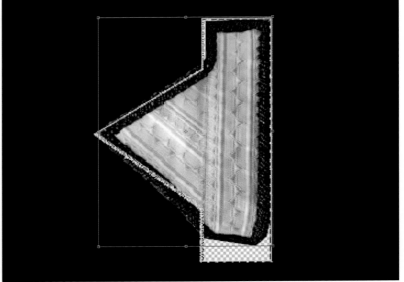

64 Use the Polygonal Lasso tool to cut out the inside of the UV snapshot. Now, select Layer 1 and go to Edit > Free Transform to roughly fit it in the UV outline.

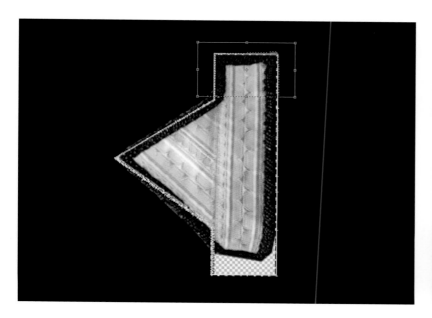

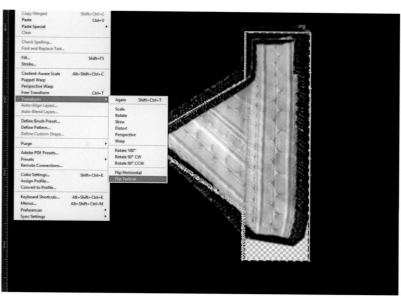

65 Use a rectangular marquee to select the top part and Edit > Free Transform to scale it to fit the UV outline.

66 Now select the top black edge, copy and paste it, Edit > Transform > Flip Vertical, and position it to roughly fit the UV outline.

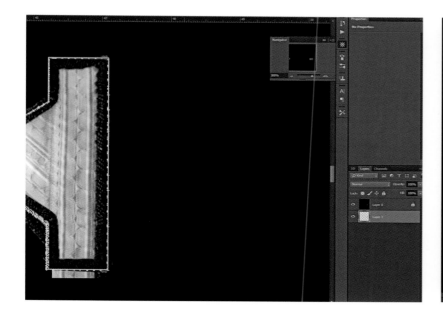

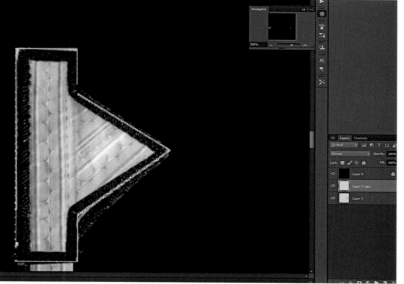

67 Copy and paste another piece to cover the rest of the empty area. Shift-select all layers in the Layers palette (not the UV snapshot (top layer)) and press [Ctrl]+[E] (PC) or [Cmd]+[E] (Mac) to flatten into one layer. Use the Clone Stamp tool to fix any issues.

68 With the newly flattened layer selected, go to Layer > Duplicate Layer and Edit > Transform > Flip Horizontal the copy. Then place it in the other cuff UV outline.

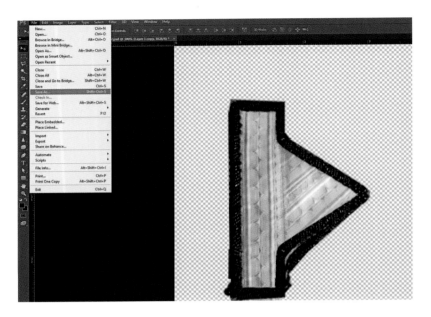

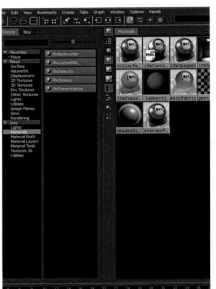

69 Save as a JPEG (and as a PSD for further work).

70 Create a new Opaque or Backscatter material, give it a file node, and load the cuff texture we just created in Photoshop.

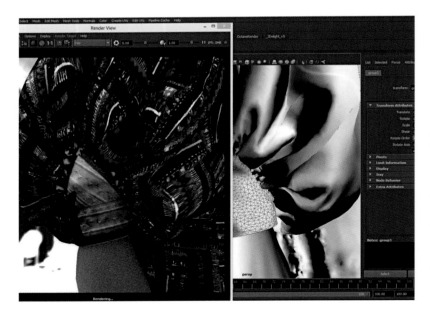

71 Select the cuffs geometry, apply the material to it, and IPR render to check that it works.

72 We now need a texture for the hat. As the reference image that we have does not contain an easily wrapable section, we will use a readily wrapped and tileable texture. Using a grey texture will allow us to tint it with a colour inside Maya more easily.

73 In Maya, select the two halves of the hat and group them.

74 Make another Opaque or Backscatter material, give it a file node, and load the hat texture.

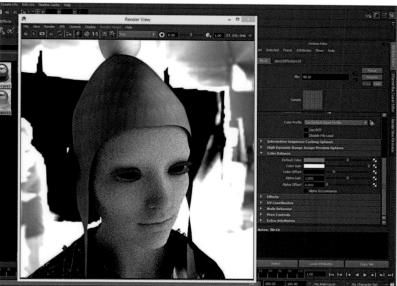

75 Apply the material to the hat and IPR render to test.

76 Double-click on the material in Hypershade and in Attribute Editor, go to Place2DTexture node and set scale (RepeatUV) to 100. In its File node, in the Color Balance section, click the Color Offset box and select a purple shade. IPR render to check.

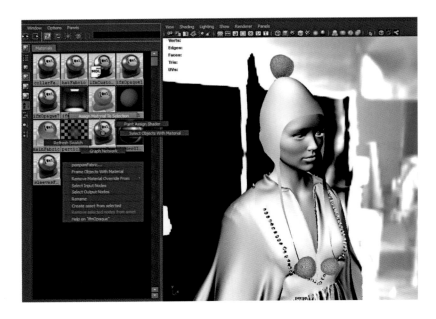

77 Create another material and apply it to the hat pom-poms. Colour it purple – no texture is necessary at this point.

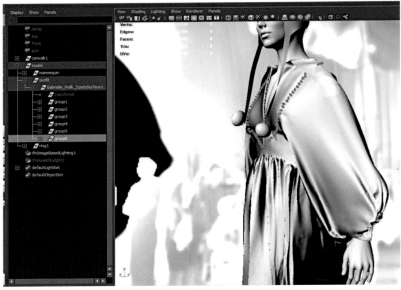

78 Select all of the mini pom-poms on the chest and group them – you may have to select them in the Outliner if selecting in the viewport is too tricky.

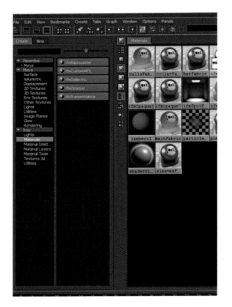

79 Create a new material, apply it to the group, and colour it purple.

80 IPR render and orbit the view to check that the material has been applied correctly.

81 In Photoshop, load the shoe texture reference, go to Edit > Perspective Warp, select an area that contains a number of whole boxes, and align it with the edges of the document.

82 Copy and paste (mirror if necessary) good areas onto problematic areas.

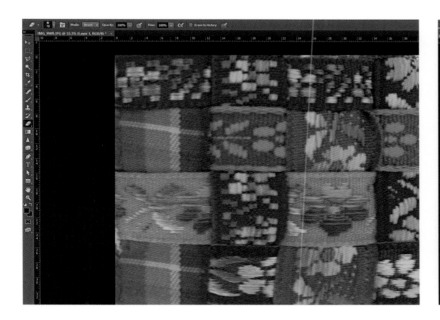

83 Use the Eraser tool if necessary with a soft brush to soften the edges of the patches – which will be in separate layers.

84 Use the Liquify filter to straighten the boxes.

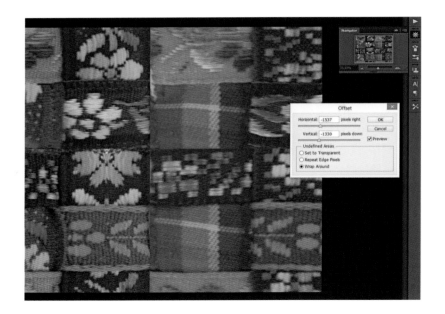

85 Crop and use the Offset filter to bring the edges/seams to the middle of the document.

86 Select the seams with rectangular marquees and drag them sideways with the Patch tool to fix them.

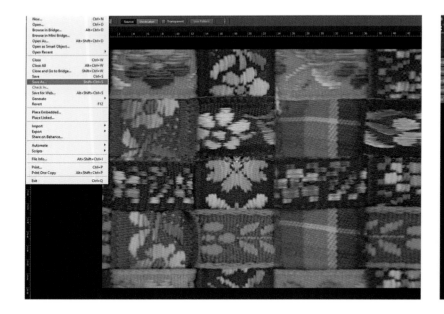

87 Save a JPEG and a PSD of the document.

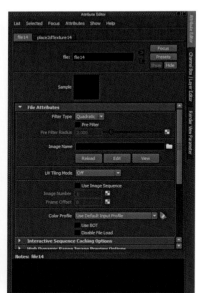

88 Make a material and apply the texture to it.

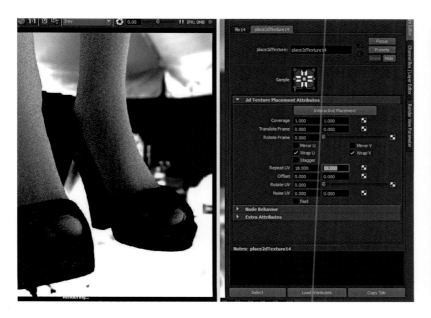

89 Select the shoe parts, group them, and apply the material to them. Change the Repeat UV attribute to scale the texture down. IPR render to confirm.

90 Select the mannequin and go to Mesh > Separate.

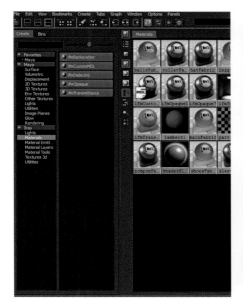

91 Create a new material and colour it purple.

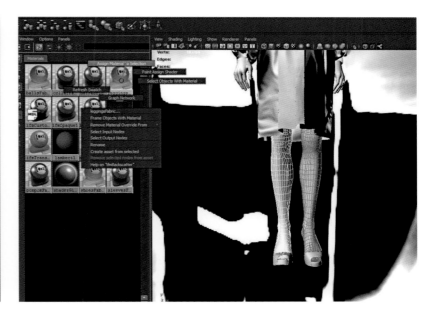

92 Select the legs, group them, and apply the material to them. IPR render to confirm.

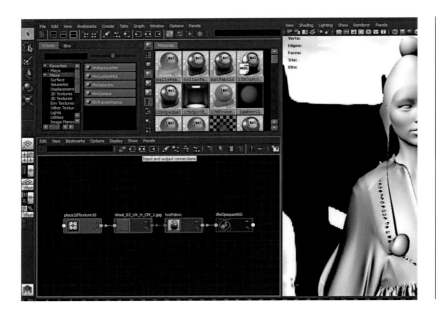

93 The next six steps are only necessary if you want to change the kind of material (opaque, backscatter etc.) but keep the rest of the components. Reset the Hypershade view, select the hat material in it, and click on the 'Input and output connectors' icon in the Node Editor. This will display all of the material's nodes.

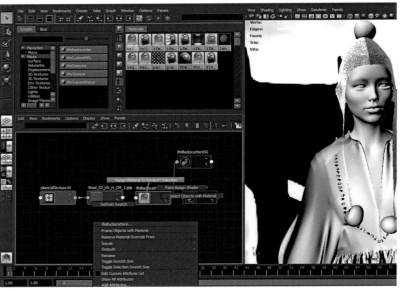

94 Select the material node (third from the left) and delete it. Create a new material in the Hypershade and apply it to the hat. Delete the spare blue shading network node. Click and drag from the output of the wool texture node to the input of the material node (select Color from the pop-up windows).

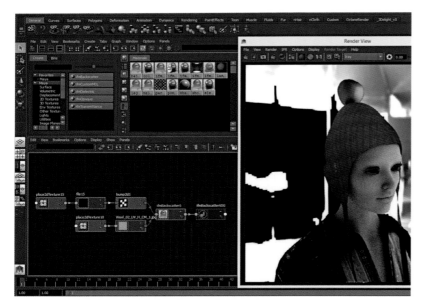

95 Double-click on the material in the Visor to see it in the Attribute Editor; in the Bump section, click on the checkered box and select File. Select the material again and click on 'Input and output connectors' to make the new nodes visible in the Visor.

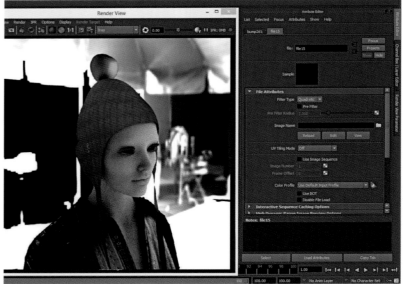

96 Double-click the File node for the bump map in the Visor, and in the Attribute Editor, click on the folder icon in the File Attributes section and load the bump texture (in this case I have chosen the same file as for the colour map).

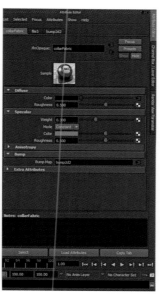

97 Do the same for the chest decoration material. This time, instead of loading another texture file, middle-mouse-drag the color map from the Node Editor into the Bump Map field in the Attribute Editor.

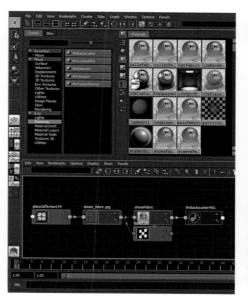

98 Do the same for the cuff and shoe materials.

99 Create an ifmCustomMDL material. These are the material presets that come with Iray for Maya. In the Attribute Editor, select 'unsupportedGifts', 'nvidia_material_examples', and 'chrome'.

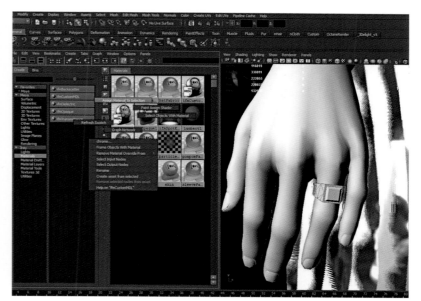

100 Select the ring and apply the material to it.

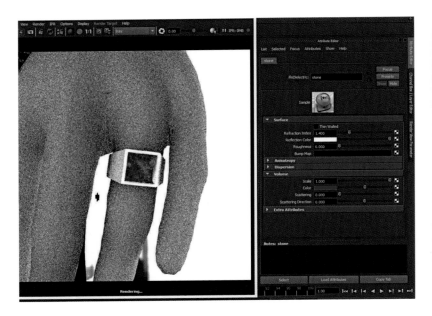

101 For the ring stone, create an ifmDielectric material, apply it to the stone geometry, and change its colour if you wish in the Volume section of the material in the Attribute Editor.

102 In the Textures 3D section of Iray, you will find ifmPerlinNoise. Select it and it will appear in the Visor. Double-click the stockings material to bring it up in the Attribute Editor, and middle-mouse-button-drag the Perlin noise texture into the bump map field.

103 Make a new ifmOpaque material and apply it to the eyes.

104 With the eyes selected, go in the UV Texture Editor, and save a UV snapshot.

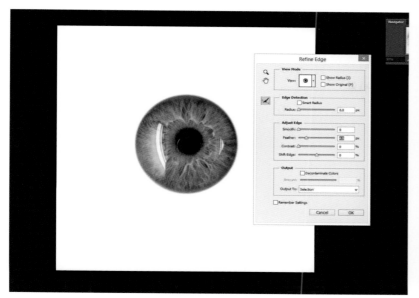

105 Source a photo of an eye (off the Internet or take your own photograph) and in Photoshop, drag a circular marquee selection around the iris. Use the Refine Edge option in the options bar to slightly feather the selection.

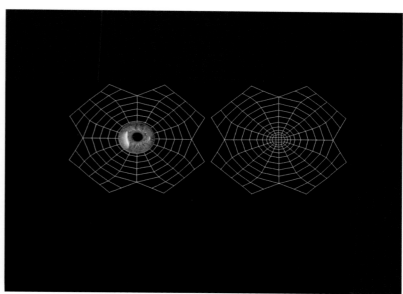

106 Load the UV snapshot for the eyes, copy the iris selection and paste it into the snapshot. Position the iris in the middle of one the eye UV maps.

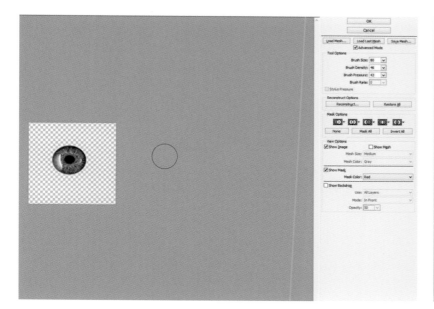

107 Drag a selection around the iris and go to Filter > Liquify. Use the liquify brush to make sure that the pupil is at the centre of the iris.

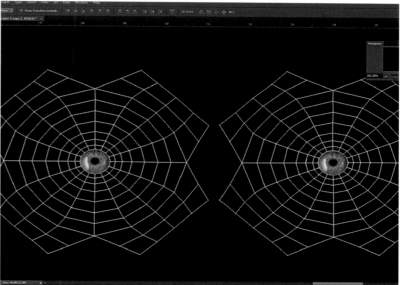

108 Duplicate the iris and place the copy at the centre of the other eye's UV map.

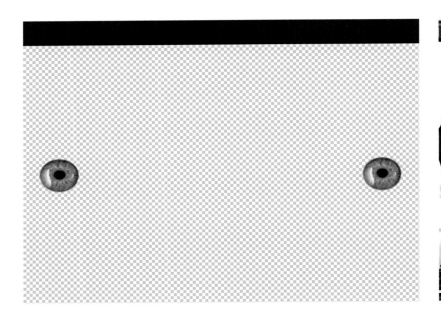

109 Make the UV background layer invisible and save the file in JPEG and PSD formats.

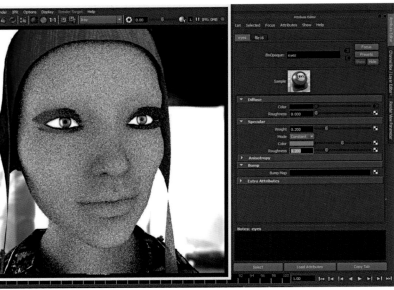

110 In Maya, double-click the eyes material, and in the Attribute Editor, in the Diffuse section, click the icon next to Color and load the eyes texture map. Under specular, set Weight and Roughness to 0.200.

111 Select the eyelids and save a UV snapshot.

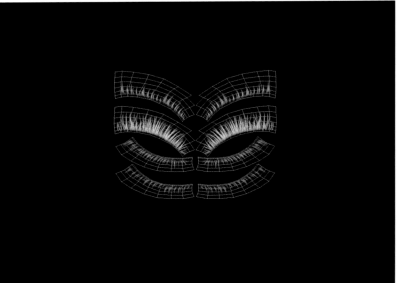

112 Open the snapshot in Photoshop, create a new layer and use a small brush with a bit of softness to paint the eyelashes as in the illustration. A graphics tablet with pen pressure is ideal for this. Remove the background and save in JPEG and PSD.

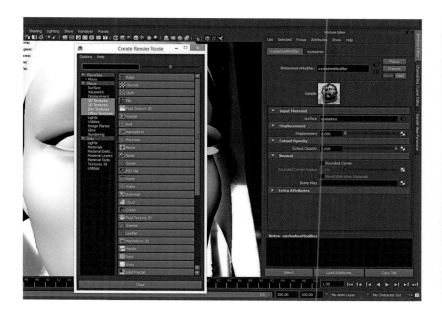

113 In Maya, pick an ifmGeometryModifier from the Hypershade and drag a new opaque material into its Surface field. In the Cutout Opacity section, click on the checkered box and select File. In the File Attributes, load the eyelashes image and make sure Alpha Is Luminance is checked in Color Balance.

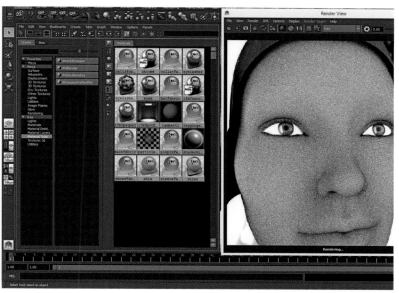

114 Apply the geometry modifier to the eyelashes geometry – in exactly the same way materials are applied.

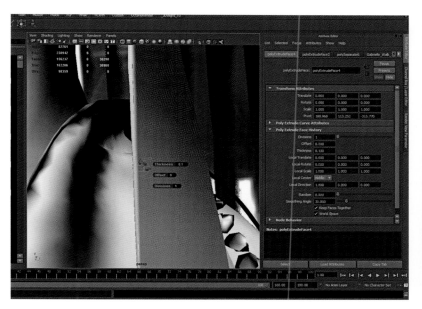

115 Select the hat geometry and go to Edit Mesh > Extrude. In the options box, go to Edit > Reset Settings and click Extrude. In the Thickness field, type in 0.1 and press [Enter]. This will give the hat thickness, making it look more realistic.

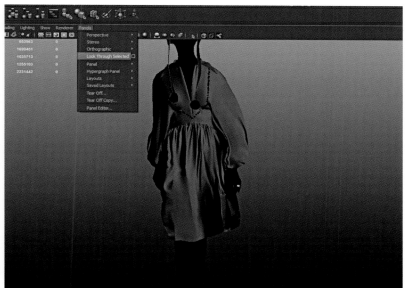

116 Go to Create > Cameras > Camera; with the camera still selected (if you deselect, you can reselect in the viewport or Outliner), in the viewport menu, select Panels > Look Through Selected. This will show the view through the selected camera.

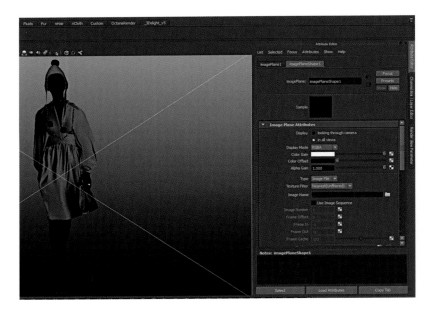

117 Move the view to see the whole mannequin, and in the Environment section of the Attribute editor, click Create to create an image plane. In the Image Plane Attributes, click on the folder next to Image Name, and load a white image – you can make one very easily in Photoshop (Edit > Select All, then Edit > Fill).

118 In the Placement section, select Fill and Fit to Resolution Gate. Also, if you want the image plane not to appear in the viewport, in the viewport menu, go to Show > Image Planes to turn it off. IPR render the camera to check that everything looks fine.

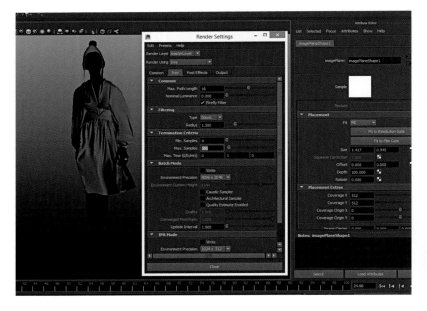

119 Open the Render Settings and set the resolution (I have gone for 2000x2667 here). Make sure the Firefly filter is on and turn the Max Samples down to 300.

120 Open the Render View, in its menu go to Render > Render and select the camera we just created. Once the render is completed, go to File > Save Image in the Render View to save the image in the desired format (I opted for JPEG here).

Retouching with Photoshop

The still renders that were previously created with IrayForMaya must now be retouched. Adobe Photoshop is used for photographic manipulation and retouching, from colour grading, to the removal of wrinkles. We will use Photoshop in this tutorial to adjust the colours, brightness and contrast of our renders, to remove imperfections, and to add photographic elements that are too difficult to create through 3D modelling. The tutorials can be downloaded from the website listed in Resources (page 173).

1 Go to Select > Color Range; using the colour picker, select a representative purple. Drag the Fuzziness slider to maximum, click OK to select the purple areas.

2 Go to Layer > New Adjustment Layer > Hue/Saturation.

3 In the New Layer options box, accept the default options.

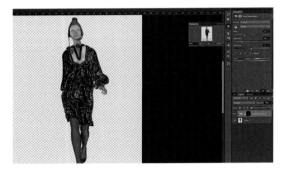

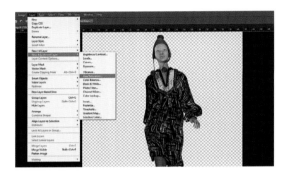

4 We now have an adjustment layer for the selection we made that can be adjusted separately. In Properties, set the Hue to -43, Saturation to -60 and Lightness to -3.

5 Go to Select > Color Range again, and this time select the yellow area on the chest.

6 Create another Hue/Saturation adjustment layer based on the selection.

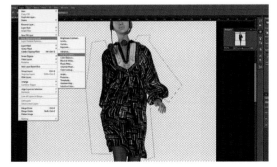

7 Set it to -5, -35 and 0.

8 Select the main layer in the Layers palette and select the patterned part of the dress with the Polygonal Lasso tool and create yet another Hue/Saturation adjustment layer.

9 Drag the Saturation down to -28.

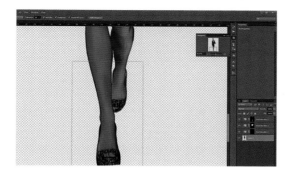

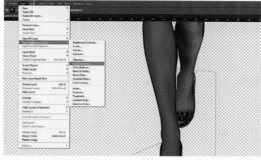

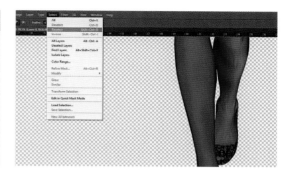

10 Select the main layer and drag a rectangular selection around the shoes.

11 Using the Quick Selection tool in 'Subtract from selection' deselect the purple areas in the rectangle. Create a Hue/Saturation layer and reduce Saturation.

12 Go to Select > Reselect to reactivate the previous selection.

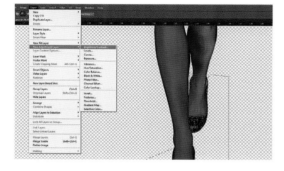

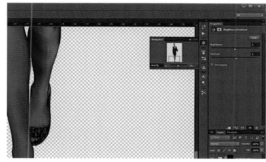

13 This time, create a Brightness/ Contrast adjustment layer.

14 Slightly increase the Contrast.

15 Some of the areas on the hat were not previously selected and so vary in brightness. Select them with the Polygonal Lasso tool.

16 Use the Clone Stamp tool to patch them up using the correctly textured areas of the hat as reference.

17 The flap is currently too thick and we must trim it. Use the Polygonal Lasso to make a selection and cut out (Edit > Cut) the excess flap.

18 Now select the excess area on the mannequin's neck.

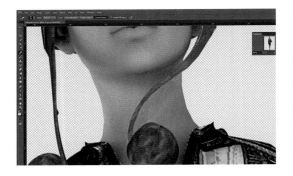  

19 Use the Clone Stamp tool and the Spot Healing Brush tool to fix the area.

20 Use the clone stamp tool to patch up the gap in the middle of the chest decoration.

21 With the Polygonal Lasso tool, select an area from the side of the decoration that contains a continuous pattern.

22 Copy and paste the area into the middle of the chest decoration.

23 Use the Eraser tool to soften the patch's edges, and set it to Darken blending mode in the Layers palette.

24 Select the main layer and the patch layer and press [Cmd]+[E] on the Mac or [Ctrl]+[E] on the PC to combine the layers.

  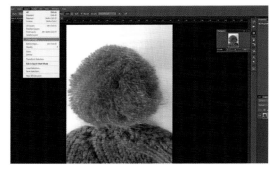

25 Use the Patch tool to fix problematic areas on the stockings.

26 Spot Healing Brush tool to fix any remaining problematic areas on the stockings.

27 Load a pom-pom photo and go to Select > Color Range.

28 In the Color Range window, select a prominent purple hue and increase the fuzziness to 200. Hit OK.

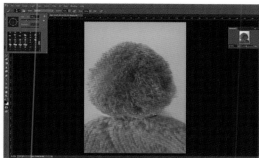

29 Click the Quick Mask icon (in toolbar below colour fields) to turn all unselected areas red. Use the Brush tool to paint the rest of the hat but not the pom-pom.

30 With an irregular brush, refine the selection by softening and randomizing the edges of the pom-pom.

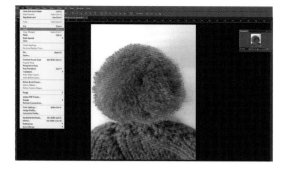

31 Get out of Quick Mask mode and copy the selection (Edit > Copy).

32 Paste the pom-pom in the main outfit document.

33 Scale the pom-pom down with the Edit > Free Transform tool.

34 Drag the pom-pom layer to the top so that it is not affected by the existing adjustment layers. Use the Eraser tool to delete the area of the pom-pom that should be hidden by the hat.

35 Use a Hue/Saturation adjustment to match the colour of the pom-pom to the colour of the hat.

36 Open the photo of the flap pom-pom and select it again with Color Range.

37 Refine the selection in Quick Mask mode, go back to normal mode, and copy the selection.

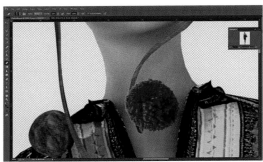

38 Paste the selection into the main document, scale it down, and position it over the placeholder 3D pom-pom that we created in Maya.

39 Duplicate the pom-pom layer, rotate and scale, and place over the other 3D pom-pom.

40 Find a photo of a fringe, select part of it with the Polygonal Lasso tool, copy and paste it into the main document, and scale it down to fit the size of the head.

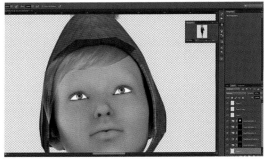

41 Select the fringe layer and turn its opacity down to 50%. This is done so we can see the layer at the back more easily.

42 Select the hat with the Quick Selection tool (make sure you are in the hat layer).

43 Select Refine Edge in the options bar, and smooth the selection. Switch to the fringe layer and delete the selected fringe area that overlaps with the hat.

44 Double-click next to the fringe layer's name in the Layers palette to get to the Layer Styles. Check Drop Shadow and play with the options to match the other shadows.

45 Use the Eraser tool with around 50% softness to trim any hard edges or corners on the fringe.

46 Use an irregular brush with the Eraser tool to make the hairs' ends look more natural. Use shape dynamics and scattering in the brush options if necessary.

47 Use the Blur tool to soften the fringe trim.

48 Adjust the fringe's colour with Image > Adjustments > Hue/Saturation if necessary.

49 Right-click on the fringe's layer in the Layers palette and select Rasterize Layer Style. This will make all layer effects (such as Drop Shadow) permanent.

50 Repeat the process (steps 40–49) for a side hairline piece.

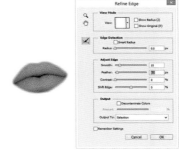

51 Draw a selection around the lips and refine its edge with the Refine Edge options.

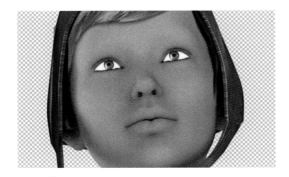

52 Add a new Hue/Saturation adjustment layer and give it a pink tint.

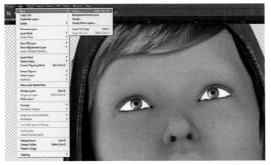

53 Go to Layer > New > Layer to create a new layer.

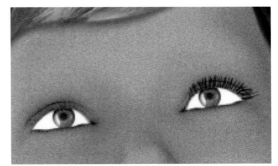

54 Use a black thin soft brush to draw some eyelashes. It is easier to do this with a graphics tablet rather than the mouse.

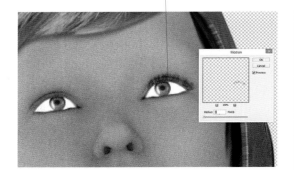

55 Use the Median filter to soften the eyelashes (Filter > Noise > Median). Use a radius of 1 and confirm.

56 Trim the eyelashes with the Eraser tool if necessary.

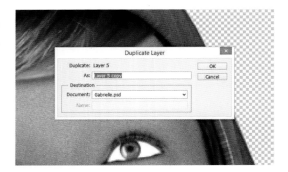

57 Go to Layer > Duplicate Layer and confirm the default options to make a copy of the eyelashes layer.

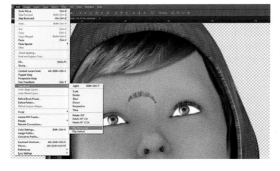

58 Go to Edit > Transform > Flip Horizontal to flip the eyelashes copy.

59 Use the Eraser to trim it if necessary.

60 Repeat steps 53–59 for the lower eyelashes and the eyebrows.

61 Use the Magic Wand selection tool to select the white areas of the eyes.

62 Select the Brush tool and a black colour and in the options bar, turn the opacity down to 10%. Paint a stroke on either side of each eye, thereby adding some shading to the white.

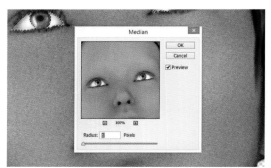

63 Use the Median filter on the shadows layer with a radius of 1 to soften it.

64 If necessary, select the irises with the Elliptical Marquee tool and move so they both look the same way. Use the Brush tool with a white colour to clear the original.

65 Use Layer > Merge Down to merge the shadows layer with the main layer.

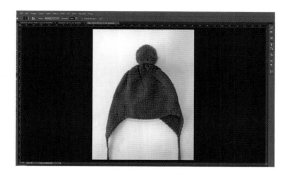

66 Load the reference photo of the hat.

67 Select the main area and refine the edge to soften it.

68 Copy the selection and paste it into the main document. Resize and place it over the 3D hat.

69 Turn the layer opacity down to 66% and set the layer style to Darken Color. Use the Eraser to trim excess texture in front of the face and around the hat.

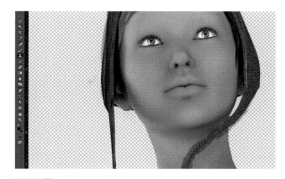

70 Use the Clone Stamp tool to extend the texture to the flaps. Use the Eraser to trim the excesses.

71 In Quick Mask mode, paint a selection over the fingernails with the Brush tool.

72 Leave Quick Mask mode and go to Select > Inverse to invert the selection.

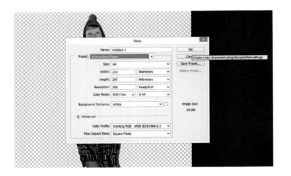

73 Go to Layer > New Adjustment Layer > Hue/Saturation.

74 Turn the Saturation and Brightness up to 10.

75 To save a document for print, go to File > New. In the options, select International Paper, and A4 (or A3) depending on the desired size.

76 Go over to the original document and flatten the layers by going to Layer > Merge Visible.

77 Go to Select > All to select the entire flattened document.

78 Go to Edit > Copy to copy it.

79 Go over to the main document and Edit > Paste.

80 Edit > Free Transform to resize the mannequin to fit in the page.

81 File > Save As and select an uncompressed format, such as BMP.

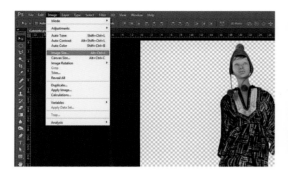

82 To save for the web, first go to Image > Image Size.

83 In the Image Size box, set the width to 1000px and the height to 1333px, make sure the resolution is set to 72 and confirm.

85 In the Save for Web dialogue, select the JPG format and a quality of 80 and click Save.

86 Make sure the format is set to 'Images Only' and save.

84 Go to File > Save for Web.

The future of 3D design

What does the future of fashion visualization hold? For one, there is a gradual movement towards real-time technologies. There are real-time cloth simulation engines that deal with live cloth simulation in video games and 3D worlds, such as Cloakworks Shroud, NVIDIA Apex, and FXGear ezCloth. Increasingly, video game engines such as Unity, Unreal and Cryengine are used for other purposes outside games. And the generation of avatars is being automated, with mobile apps being used for single view measurements of bodies. Poikos is one of them. This means that in the not too distant future, we will be able to scan our bodies and use them in a real-time virtual environment.

There have also been advances in the realistic physics and appearance of fabrics, which can now be modeled as structures of yarns with what is called Structural Modelling Software. Companies such as EAT (DesignScope) and TexEng use this technique.

There have also been great leaps in the fields of holography, stereography and projections. Musion, for example, is an agency that provides 3D holographic projection for live events. Stefan Eckert collaborated with designer Tim Jockel and director Florian Sigl to create the world's first complete 3D holographic fashion show. Project Omote is a real-time face tracking and projection mapping collaboration between media artist Nobumichi Asai, makeup artist Hiroto Kuwahara, and French digital image engineer Paul Lacroix. And there are increasing numbers of designers making use of 3D and projections. Jean Paul Gaultier has used them; Alexander McQueen's Fall/Winter 2006 Paris Fashion Week show featured a hologram of Kate Moss; Burberry also ran a holographic catwalk show in Beijing in 2011.

There have also been developments in virtual reality in the shape of Oculus Rift, a virtual reality headset, and Leap Motion, a hands movement sensor. These are devices that can enhance 3D experiences, such as virtual stores and curation – for example the Valentino Garavani Museum and Stylmee Shop City. On the other hand, point-of-sale installations in physical stores are also changing, such as the virtual mirrors that were trialled in John Lewis.

Resources

Tutorial files
www.3Dfashionvisualization.com

Additional tutorials
www.lynda.com
www.digitaltutors.com
www.simplymaya.com

Blender
www.blender.org
www.blender.org/support/tutorials

Clo3D
www.clo3d.com

Daz
www.daz3d.com
www.daz3d.com/help/help-daz-3d-video-tutorials

Illustrator
www.adobe.com/uk/products/illustrator.html
success.adobe-education.com

IrayForMaya
www.0x1-software.com/en/produkte/0x1-irayformaya.html
www.0x1-software.com/en/produkte/0x1-irayformaya/tutorial.html

Marvelous Designer
www.marvelousdesigner.com
www.marvelousdesigner.com/learn/lessons

Maya
www.autodesk.co.uk/products/maya/overview
www.autodesk.com/education/free-software/maya

Octane
www.render.otoy.com
www.render.otoy.com/shop/standalone_edu.php

Optitex
www.optitex.com/en/Pattern-Design-Software
www.optitex.com/en/webinars
www.optitex.com/Help/en/index.php/
PDS:Getting_Started_With_OptiTex_PDS

Photoshop
www.photoshop.com
success.adobe-education.com

Rhino
www.rhino3d.com/download
www.rhino3d.com/edu

V-Stitcher
www.browzwear.com/products/v-stitcher/#1

Picture credits

Original fashion design by Anne Valerie Hash:
pages 18, 48, 58
Original fashion design by Raphaëlle Mura: pages
20, 47
Original fashion design by Boudicca: pages 59, 72
Original fashion design by Gabrielle Miller: pages
103, 120, 124, 143, 159, 160
p103 ©catwalking.com

Glossary

3D Geometry / 3D Mesh The polygons that form a 3D object, without any maps applied to them.

Bump Map A greyscale 2D bitmap which, when applied to a 3D mesh, gives the illusion of details on the surface.

Cache/Maya Cache A file that describes the translation (movement) of a 3D mesh's vertices over time, thereby animating the mesh.

CAD/CAM Computer Aided Design/ Computer Aided Manufacturing

Cloth Simulation The process of making a 3D mesh behave like a piece of cloth, usually through spring-based physics.

Collada An open interchange file format for interactive 3D applications. It supports animation.

Diffuse Map A 2D bitmap that describes the variations of colour over a 3D mesh.

Displacement Map A 2D bitmap that gives a 3D mesh details too minute to model by manipulating polygons.

FBX A proprietary interchange file format for interactive 3D applications, owned by Autodesk. It supports animation.

GPU Rendering Rendering carried out by the Graphics Processing Unit (graphics card) of a computer, rather than by its CPU (Central Processing Unit).

HDRI Lighting High Dynamic Range Image Lighting lights up a 3D scene based on brightness and colour variations over a 32-bit bitmap.

IPR Interactive Photorealistic Rendering

Iray NVidia's interactive, physically based rendering technology.

Manipulator / Gizmo The main tool with which 3D objects can be manipulated in the viewports of a 3D design program.

OBJ A geometry definition file format. It does not support animation.

Plugin A piece of software that accompanies or enhances a larger host program (for example, Iray for Maya).

Rendering The process of converting a 3D scene into a 2D bitmap, by taking into account cameras, objects, materials and lights.

Scene Hierarchy This is a diagram of the contents of a 3D scene, describing the relationships between its objects.

Shader A set of commands that create a material with which meshes can be shaded.

Specular Map A 2D bitmap that describes the variations of shininess over a 3D mesh.

Texture Map A 2D bitmap that increases a mesh's detail through colour, shininess, transparency.

Transparency Map A 2D bitmap that describes the variations of transparency over a 3D mesh.

UV Coordinates The coordinates that define a 2D texture map's position and scale on a 3D mesh.

World/Local Coordinates The absolute coordinates (x, y, z) of a 3D scene, and relative coordinates of the individual objects contained in the scene.

Index

Index